New Daylight

Edited by Naomi Starkey   September–December 2009

Suggestions for using *New Daylight*

Find a regular time and place, if possible, where you can read and pray undisturbed. Before you begin, take time to be still and perhaps use the BRF prayer. Then read the Bible passage slowly (try reading it aloud if you find it over-familiar), followed by the comment. You can also use *New Daylight* for group study and discussion, if you prefer.

The prayer or point for reflection can be a starting point for your own meditation and prayer. Many people like to keep a journal to record their thoughts about a Bible passage and items for prayer. In *New Daylight* we also note the Sundays and some of the special festivals from the Church calendar, to keep in step with the Christian year.

New Daylight and the Bible

New Daylight contributors use a range of Bible versions, and you will find a list of the versions used in each issue at the back of the notes on page 154. You are welcome to use your own preferred version alongside the passage printed in the notes, and this can be particularly helpful if the Bible text has been abridged.

New Daylight affirms that the whole of the Bible is God's revelation to us, and we should read, reflect on and learn from every part of both Old and New Testaments. Usually the printed comment presents a straightforward 'thought for the day', but sometimes it may also raise questions rather than simply providing answers, as we wrestle with some of the more difficult passages of Scripture.

New Daylight *is also available in a deluxe edition (larger format). Check out your local Christian bookshop or contact the BRF office, who can also give more details about a cassette version for the visually impaired. For a Braille edition, contact St John's Guild, 8 St Raphael's Court, Avenue Road, St Albans, AL1 3EH.*

Writers in this issue

Amy Boucher Pye is an American who has lived in the UK for over a decade. She makes her home in North London with her husband and young family and enjoys writing for Christian periodicals, including *Quiet Spaces, Woman Alive* and *Christian Marketplace*.

Rachel Boulding is Deputy Editor of the *Church Times*. Before this, she was Senior Liturgy Editor at Church House Publishing. She lives in Dorset with her husband and son—and, during school terms, more than 70 teenage boys.

Margaret Silf is an ecumenical Christian, committed to working across and beyond the denominational divides. She devotes herself to writing and accompanying others on their spiritual journey.

David Winter is retired from parish ministry. An honorary Canon of Christ Church, Oxford, he is well known as a writer and broadcaster. His most recent book for BRF is *Pilgrim's Way*.

Tony Horsfall is a freelance trainer based in Yorkshire, where he is an elder of his local church. He regularly leads retreats and Quiet Days in this country and overseas. His latest book for BRF is *Mentoring for Spiritual Growth*.

Naomi Starkey is the editor of *New Daylight*. She also edits *Quiet Spaces*, BRF's prayer and spirituality journal, as well as commissioning BRF's range of books for adults.

Helen Julian CSF is an Anglican Franciscan sister, currently serving her community as Minister Provincial. She has written *Living the Gospel* and *The Road to Emmaus* for BRF.

David Robertson has ministered in a variety of parishes since his ordination in 1979 and is currently a vicar in Halifax. He has written *Marriage—Restoring Our Vision* and *Collaborative Ministry* for BRF.

John Proctor is married to Elaine, with two adult children. He works for the United Reformed Church, teaching the New Testament in Cambridge and b. John has written *PBC Matthew* (BRF, 2001) and booklets on the Gospels and Acts in the Grove Biblical Series.

Adrian Plass is an popular writer and speaker in many countries. His most recent books for BRF are *When You Walk* (revised and expanded) and *Blind Spots in the Bible*.

Further BRF reading for this issue

For more in-depth coverage of some of the passages in these Bible reading notes, we recommend the following titles:

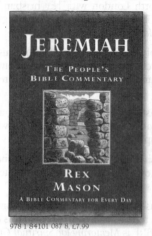

JEREMIAH

THE PEOPLE'S BIBLE COMMENTARY

REX MASON

A BIBLE COMMENTARY FOR EVERY DAY

978 1 84101 087 8, £7.99

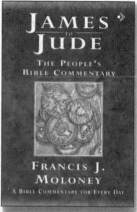

JAMES *to* **JUDE**

THE PEOPLE'S BIBLE COMMENTARY

FRANCIS J. MOLONEY

A BIBLE COMMENTARY FOR EVERY DAY

978 1 84101 092 2, £7.99

GALATIANS *and* **1&2 THESSALONIANS**

THE PEOPLE'S BIBLE COMMENTARY

JOHN FENTON

A BIBLE COMMENTARY FOR EVERY DAY

978 1 84101 012 0, £7.99

PROVERBS

THE PEOPLE'S BIBLE COMMENTARY

ENID B. MELLOR

A BIBLE COMMENTARY FOR EVERY DAY

978 1 84101 071 7, £7.99

Naomi Starkey writes...

Perhaps more than usual, our readings in this issue of *New Daylight* are linked into the Church calendar, the pattern of festivals and commemorations that explore the themes of Christian faith over the course of the year. While many churches delight to follow this pattern, others have deliberately abandoned it, finding it for various reasons too confining for their worship. And, of course, a good many *New Daylight* readers belong to denominations that have traditionally not kept such patterns, and may find it all a bit baffling!

For those less familiar with the Church calendar, it is worth bearing in mind that within its seasons there is a constant 'mini-emphasis' on Fridays as a day for quieter reflection, an echo of the fact that Jesus died on a Friday. At the same time, every Sunday is in some sense an Easter Day, when people gather to praise God for all he has done for us through his Son. The other special days and times provide an overarching structure of meaning and symbolism, beginning in Advent.

Following this calendar can be a useful balance against the pressures of a consumer society. After all, why should we start thinking about Easter eggs in January or Christmas preparations in September? Keeping Advent—even if we do no more than light a candle each week at church—can remind us that the coming of Jesus followed centuries of watching and waiting by God's people. All too easily, the stress of present-buying, carol services, nativity plays and food preparation can mean that we wake on Christmas morning with little peace of mind or sense of what we are celebrating (and I speak from experience).

For specific daily Advent readings I should direct you to this year's BRF Advent book, *Shock and Awe* by Ian Coffey, but in this *New Daylight* we are drawing attention to some other highlights of the Church calendar at this time of year. We have readings by David Robertson on Christ the King (celebrated on the Sunday before Advent) and meditations on the cross by Rachel Boulding around Holy Cross Day (14 September)—and I have written some readings for All Saints and All Souls, a reflective time of year which has been swept away in public consciousness by the opportunity to buy witches' hats, fright masks and plastic skeletons.

The BRF Prayer

Almighty God,
you have taught us that your word is a lamp for our feet
and a light for our path. Help us, and all who prayerfully
read your word, to deepen our fellowship with each other
through your love. And in so doing may we come to know you
more fully, love you more truly, and follow more faithfully in
the steps of your son Jesus Christ, who lives and reigns with
you and the Holy Spirit, one God for evermore. Amen.

Psalm 18: The Lord is my rock

September is a time of new beginnings for many, with those going back to school and others embarking on a healthy eating plan after the excess of summer holidays! Often we rush forward with new ventures, but it is wise and fitting to slow down in our Bible reading and take a meditative approach. This we are doing as we spend a week and a half on Psalm 18.

This is David's song in which he gives thanks for deliverance from his enemies, including the persecuting Saul. It appears almost identically in the historical account of David's life in 2 Samuel 22 and comes just before his final words. It is called a royal psalm as it would have accompanied the liturgy used in the temple when a king was present. The overarching theme is thanksgiving to God, the rock who saves.

David spent a lot of time on the run from Saul and, through this crucible of testing and hardship, his faith in and love for the living Lord grew firm and solid. As he recounts God's saving acts, he gives all the glory to God for helping him escape, keeping him hidden and giving him victory. He speaks of the Lord's holiness and might, his anger at injustice, his love and care for his children in trouble.

Some of the images will be foreign to us: what, for instance, is the horn of salvation? (A symbol of power and strength, animal horns were used for anointing with oil or carrying other liquids in battle.) Even transporting ourselves back to biblical times and geography can be a stretch as we try to visualize the rocks and crags David hid in or the stark desert sands. Employing our imaginations and delving into the text, however, is rewarding and enriching and helps us in our worship of God. As we savour the images, we can ask God through his Holy Spirit to bring his word to life in our imaginations.

This psalm has five sections: an opening of praise, the story of how God saved David, verses on instruction in righteousness, a description of victory and a concluding praise to God. We won't skip any of the verses as we join David and his descendents to give thanks to the Lord—our refuge, redeemer, shield and deliverer. Praise be to God, our rock and saviour!

Amy Boucher Pye

7

My rock and refuge

I love you, Lord, my strength. The Lord is my rock, my fortress and my deliverer; my God is my rock, in whom I take refuge, my shield and the horn of my salvation, my stronghold. I called to the Lord, who is worthy of praise, and I have been saved from my enemies.

Our psalm begins with an impassioned cri de coeur: 'I love you, Lord!' David's adoration and thanksgiving pours out in an intimate declaration. These are the words of lovers, of parents and children, of closest friends. They are also the words of an earthly king spoken to the heavenly King who rescued him from his enemies.

David employs seven metaphors to describe the saving nature of God: Yahweh is his rock, fortress, deliverer, refuge, shield, horn of salvation and stronghold. These images relate to both the military battles David fought throughout his life and how God provided him with physical safety as he hid from his pursuers, swords drawn and ready to strike. When he was in danger, he called to the Lord for help.

We may not need to take cover in mountain hideaways, but God wants to be our rock—our firm foundation. With him, the building of our lives will withstand powerful and dangerous storms. As Paul said to the Ephesians, we have been 'built on the foundation of the apostles and prophets, with Christ Jesus himself as the chief cornerstone. In him the whole building is joined together and rises to become a holy temple in the Lord' (2:20–21). Indeed, God yearns to be our stronghold and fortress.

In David's time, a fortress was a remote rocky spot that was used as a place of refuge. Its very isolation provided a safe haven. Today, too, the unchanging God outstretches his arms and welcomes us to shelter in his presence. As Jesus says in Matthew 11:28, 'Come to me, all you who are weary and burdened, and I will give you rest.'

A rock to build our lives on. A fortress for protection. Delivery, safety, refuge and strength. These are all attributes of the God who loves us and draws us to himself.

Prayer

Lord, help me build my life on your foundation. Shield me this day from those who would oppress me. Hide me in the shadows of your wings. I love you!

ABP

Deadly cords and snares

The cords of death entangled me; the torrents of destruction overwhelmed me. The cords of the grave coiled around me; the snares of death confronted me. In my distress I called to the Lord; I cried to my God for help. From his temple he heard my voice; my cry came before him, into his ears. The earth trembled and quaked, and the foundations of the mountains shook; they trembled because he was angry.

As David continues his song of thanksgiving, he recounts how God has saved him. His imagery is gripping: death, destruction and the grave. He speaks of the ensnaring cords that circled him, trapped him and knocked him to his knees. The torrents of destruction spark images of floods of rushing, swirling, deadly water.

In that desperate situation, he called to the Lord for help and his voice was not ignored. Yahweh heard the cry of the oppressed. He who is all-powerful and all-holy makes the earth tremble through his anger at injustice. The Lord wants to save us from any such binding cords. They may be the pain of a friend's betrayal, disease that wastes the body and taxes the mind, the depression that feels like a suffocating cloak or the fear of failure, a crippling lack of self-confidence or an addiction of some kind.

In our fallen world there aren't always easy answers to the litany of the snares of death. We should remember, though, that our God is the champion of his people, whether or not the cords are of our making. He's not locked away in a distant palace—when we cry out, as David did, our voices reach his ears and he responds. Sometimes he shakes the earth with his anger, like Jesus raging against those selling cattle and exchanging money in the temple. At other times, he is a rock in turbulent conditions, as we saw yesterday. He sends healing, like that heralded by the prophets Isaiah and Jeremiah (see Isaiah 58:8 or Jeremiah 33:6) or that enacted by Jesus as he healed the lepers or the haemorrhaging woman (Luke 17:11–19; 8:43–48).

Like David, we can cry out to God, for he hears us and will free us from our cords of death.

Prayer

Lord, the waters are rushing over me. Come and rescue me; hear my cry.

ABP

Holy, holy, holy is the Lord God Almighty

Smoke rose from his nostrils; consuming fire came from his mouth, burning coals blazed out of it. He parted the heavens and came down; dark clouds were under his feet. He mounted the cherubim and flew; he soared on the wings of the wind. He made darkness his covering, his canopy around him—the dark rain clouds of the sky. Out of the brightness of his presence clouds advanced, with hailstones and bolts of lightning.

As David tells of God's deliverance, he uses powerful images to show how Yahweh manifests himself to his people. We see God's anger at evil and sin through the smoke, consuming fire and burning coals. Fire, and especially consuming fire, is a common metaphor in the Bible. It purifies and cleanses all that is not holy as it dispels the darkness. Like the fiery sun, it is the source of life.

Though holy to the core, God, in his graciousness, hides himself in the dark clouds, for his presence would overwhelm us. We who are sinful cannot stand before him unaided. Even hidden, his brightness shines through.

God's holiness is an attribute that we often dismiss, ignore or dilute today. For instance, we may fail to name sin when it pervades our lives. It may be systemic evil, such as racism or classism, that we disregard. It may be our 'harmless gossip' at church or the school gates. It may be a root of bitterness to which we cling. We so easily compromise, rationalize and liberalize. God, though, calls us to be holy as he is holy. Through his Holy Spirit he enables us to live a life of righteousness, truth and love. As the apostle Paul wrote to the Galatians, 'Those who belong to Christ Jesus have crucified the sinful nature with its passions and desires' (Galatians 5:24). He will give us the resources we need to be holy and stand up for truth with a spirit of grace. Out of this will flow his life-affirming gifts: 'the fruit of the Spirit is love, joy, peace, patience, kindness, goodness, faithfulness, gentleness and self-control' (vv. 22–23).

Prayer

'Therefore, since we are receiving a kingdom that cannot be shaken, let us be thankful, and so worship God acceptably with reverence and awe, for our "God is a consuming fire"' (Hebrews 12:28–29).

ABP

Search and rescue

The Lord thundered from heaven; the voice of the Most High resounded. He shot his arrows and scattered the enemy, with great bolts of lightning he routed them. The valleys of the sea were exposed and the foundations of the earth laid bare at your rebuke, Lord, at the blast of breath from your nostrils. He reached down from on high and took hold of me; he drew me out of deep waters. He rescued me from my powerful enemy, from my foes, who were too strong for me. They confronted me in the day of my disaster, but the Lord was my support.

The power and might of Yahweh continue to dominate David's song of thanksgiving and commentators believe that David here is alluding to previous acts of God. The description of God moving the waters of the sea probably refers to the parting of the Red Sea when the Israelites fled from Egypt (see Exodus 14) and when they crossed the Jordan River as they entered the Promised Land (see Joshua 3).

In referring to these acts of deliverance, David is saying that the God of his fathers—Abraham, Moses and Joshua—is his God, too, and he has saved him on an equally mighty scale. David makes the song personal when he tells how Yahweh reached down and rescued him from the deep waters that threatened to overwhelm him. His foes were too strong, but the saving God intervened.

As you pray through this psalm today, take a moment to wonder at the power of the Lord who loves us. Put yourself in David's shoes as you imagine him thinking back to God's liberating rescue. Allow yourself to marvel at God's mighty acts, like the moving and halting of the waters from the sea to allow his chosen people a pathway to escape.

God is no less powerful today. As we cry out to him, he will lovingly send down a search and rescue team to scoop us out of the waters that threaten to overcome us.

Prayer

Lord Jesus, we sometimes forget your power, as did the disciples who cowered in the boat as the waters raged around them, but you still calmed the storm in an instant. Help us to look to you to bring peace in the storms of our lives.

ABP

A spacious place

He brought me out into a spacious place; he rescued me because he delighted in me. The Lord has dealt with me according to my righteousness; according to the cleanness of my hands he has rewarded me. For I have kept the ways of the Lord; I am not guilty of turning from my God.

I don't think I'm claustrophobic, but I can readily imagine David's relief when the living Lord led him from his cramped hiding place in the rocks and crags out to a spacious place. I love being out in the wide world of creation, especially beside an ocean. The pounding surf at the shoreline provides a rich introduction to the vast waters that stretch as far as the eye can see. As I gaze out, I find deep peace and rest.

Maybe that oceanside view is one you behold regularly, but for me it's more of a rarity. I have to seek the Lord's spacious place in the stuff of my own daily life, such as my light and sunny study in our Victorian vicarage, the freedom I feel after meeting a deadline or my joy at glimpsing a bubble floating up outside my window, courtesy of my toddler and our au pair, as I did just now.

Of course, the most spacious place we can find is in knowing the love and affirmation of our heavenly Father. Taking some images from scripture, we are his beautiful one (Song of Solomon 2:13), a lily among thorns (v. 2) and the apple of his eye (Psalm 17:8) or, as Moses said in blessing the Israelites as they entered the promised land, 'The eternal God is your refuge, and underneath are the everlasting arms' (Deuteronomy 33:27).

Whatever our circumstances, God will take us to a spacious place. As we look to him, we can leave behind the need to acquire more stuff, more deadlines or deals or more friends on Facebook. He will comfort us in our grief and bind up our wounds. He reaches out through Jesus and (in the words of the verse we pondered a few days ago) says, 'Come to me, all you who are weary and burdened, and I will give you rest' (Matthew 11:28).

Prayer

Father, I give you my fears, desires and dreams. Take me to your spacious place, that I might be set free to love and serve you.

ABP

Righteousness and faithfulness

All his laws are before me; I have not turned away from his decrees. I have been blameless before him and have kept myself from sin. The Lord has rewarded me according to my righteousness, according to the cleanness of my hands in his sight. To the faithful you show yourself faithful, to the blameless you show yourself blameless, to the pure you show yourself pure, but to the devious you show yourself shrewd. You save the humble but bring low those whose eyes are haughty.

As we read these verses (and, indeed, verses 19–21 from yesterday), we might want to ask, 'Excuse me, David? What about sleeping with Bathsheba and getting her husband killed? That's 'blameless' behaviour?

David's song seems to illustrate a more general principle, however—namely that, if we follow God's ways, he will protect and prosper us. After all, David suffered the consequences of his big mistake, just as we often endure trials when we turn from God's commands.

We need to tread carefully here. Although God may allow suffering in response to our sins, sometimes things go amiss even though we've done no wrong, such as happened to Job or the man born blind (see John 9:3). Sometimes those who do evil still prosper. Generally, however, I believe that the original principle holds true.

We can look to Psalm 1 for an affirmation of this. In it we read of the wicked who are like chaff and the wind blows them away, but also of those who delight in the law of the Lord and 'are like a tree planted by streams of water, which yields its fruit in season and whose leaf does not wither—whatever they do prospers' (v. 3).

Although David was not without sin, God still called him 'a man after my own heart' (Acts 13:22). He made mistakes, but came back time and again to seek forgiveness and be put on the right track. Like David, no matter what our sins are, we can be made righteous, clean, faithful, blameless, pure and humble.

Prayer

'Create in me a clean heart, O God, and renew a right spirit within me. Cast me not away from your presence, and take not your Holy Spirit from me. Restore to me the joy of your salvation, and uphold me with a willing spirit'
(Psalm 51:10–12, ESV).

ABP

God, our source

You, Lord, keep my lamp burning; my God turns my darkness into light. With your help I can advance against a troop; with my God I can scale a wall.

As David recounts the works of God, he acknowledges that everything comes from the Lord—oil for his lamp, military help, strength to climb a wall. His song rises out of many years of trusting God and seeing him deliver, whether it was when David defeated Goliath with God's help, five stones and a sling or the Lord gave him a hiding place from Saul.

These testing times provided David with a choice: he could trust God to take him through the difficulties or else blame him because things weren't going to plan. As we've seen, David wasn't perfect, but he learned from his mistakes and sought God. After a lifetime of seeing God make good on his promises, he wants to attribute all the glory and honour to him.

Our world is so different from David's. We have the conveniences of modern life, such as travel, communication and technology. With all of these things making our lives easier (but more complicated), we can be tempted to think that we control our lives. If our hearts are tender towards God, we see that he is the source of all that we have and do. Sometimes, however, we only turn to God as a last resort because of disaster, calamity or sickness.

How can we follow David's lead in attributing all the glory to the Lord? Perhaps it is in offering to God that misunderstanding with a friend. We can seek his wisdom when our children go off the rails. We can ask him to help us see that annoying person as he sees them. We can say thank you when we complete a project, have a joyous time with a loved one or make it to our destination safely.

God's help is as present today as it was for David. As we trust in him moment by moment, we, too, will be able to say that he has provided for our needs and turned our darkness into light.

Prayer

'Yours, Lord, is the greatness and the power and the glory and the majesty and the splendour, for everything in heaven and earth is yours' (1 Chronicles 29:11).

ABP

Rock of ages

As for God, his way is perfect: the Lord's word is flawless; he shields all who take refuge in him. For who is God besides the Lord? And who is the Rock except our God?

Today, David again calls God the rock who provides him with refuge. It may seem repetitive, but, as Charles Spurgeon said in *The Treasury of David*, 'Second thoughts upon God's mercy should be and often are the best'.

As Moses was preparing the Israelites to go into the Promised Land, he sang a song about the Lord and used words very similar to David's: 'He is the Rock, his works are perfect' (Deuteronomy 32:4). Clearly God as the rock, sure foundation and provider of refuge was an important image to our heroes in the faith.

In the desert lands of the Bible, rocks were a welcome sight as they would provide shade from the scorching heat of the sun. Under their overhang, the desert creatures and plants flourished and a weary traveller could find shelter, rest and perhaps even a spring of water. Rocks were also the foundation for the fortresses that would provide safety from attacking troops.

The image of the rock is important in the New Testament, too. Jesus says that those who put his teachings into practice are like 'a wise man who built his house on the rock' (Matthew 7:24). Though the elements raged against it, it didn't fall. Also, Jesus renamed Simon 'Peter', the Greek word for rock, saying, 'and on this rock I will build my church' (16:18).

God wants to be the foundation of our lives. He is filled with the strength that does not waver and a solidity that will not crack. As we look to him for help, he will provide shelter and refreshment. The need might be financial—negative equity on a mortgage or out-of-control fuel prices. The need might be emotional—for someone to love and be loved by. It might be physical—for healing and restoration. He will provide answers—perhaps not as we would, but according to his mercy and wisdom, for his way is perfect and his word is flawless.

Prayer

Lord God, you are the rock of our lives, a mighty fortress who never fails. We look to you for shelter, rest and refreshment.

ABP

Boot camp

It is God who arms me with strength and keeps my way secure. He makes my feet like the feet of a deer; he causes me to stand on the heights. He trains my hands for battle; my arms can bend a bow of bronze. You make your saving help my shield, and your right hand sustains me; your help has made me great. You provide a broad path for my feet, so that my ankles do not give way.

Have you ever twisted your ankle? I did once when on a wilderness adventure in northern Minnesota as we were trekking across the Grand Portage with canoes and packs on our backs. The ground was wet and, for some silly reason, we made the epic journey (some nine miles) at night. After many hours, I slipped and fell. Although the backpack provided a cushion, my ankle contorted unnaturally. I felt every painful step.

As Christians, we may trip and fall, but, as we follow God, he will make our way secure. So says David, who turns his song of thanksgiving into a personal litany of the ways in which God has helped him. With God, he has the grace and surety of a deer in a high place (a feeling that I would have appreciated on that slippery trail!) Again, Yahweh is his saving help, shield and sustenance, the one who provides a wide path for his feet.

One of the commentators likens these verses to a 'boot camp for warriors', similar to the spiritual armour that Paul outlines to the Ephesians (such as the belt of truth, breastplate of righteousness and shield of faith). We may not have to rout our enemies, but we do battle against the 'spiritual forces of evil in the heavenly realms' (Ephesians 6:12).

May I extend a rallying call to you to take up your shield against the fiery darts of the enemy, whether they be words of discouragement or an insipid disbelief in the power of the almighty God. Call on the Lord and he will train your arms as you hold the sword of the Spirit—the word of God—while praying for all the saints.

Prayer

Lord, you are my shield, defender, strength and security. Your right hand sustains me and you provide a broad path for my feet. Train me to serve and love you.

ABP

Just war?

I pursued my enemies and overtook them; I did not turn back till they were destroyed. I crushed them so that they could not rise; they fell beneath my feet. You armed me with strength for battle; you humbled my adversaries before me. You made my enemies turn their backs in flight, and I destroyed my foes. They cried for help, but there was no one to save them—to the Lord, but he did not answer. I beat them as fine as windblown dust; I trampled them like mud in the streets. You have delivered me from the attacks of the people; you have made me the head of nations. People I did not know now serve me, foreigners cower before me; as soon as they hear of me, they obey me. They all lose heart; they come trembling from their strongholds.

When I first agreed to write these notes on Psalm 18, I thought it was a wonderful psalm to delve into, but I didn't want to write on the above verses. They are just so graphic: the destroying of foes, them being beaten into dust, trampled in the mud. Not exactly refreshing morning reading.

I looked to the commentaries for some help, but they seemed to skip over this section. Gleason L. Archer's *New International Encyclopedia of Bible Difficulties* (Zondervan, 2001), though, gave me some insight. He makes a compelling argument for the right of law-abiding citizens to self-defence. As he says, 'How could God be called "good" if He forbade His people to protect their wives from ravishment and strangulation… or to resist invaders who have come to pick up their children and dash out their brains against the wall'? (p. 219). These are graphic images, I know, but, because we live in a fallen world that often doesn't follow God's rules, we need to face up to these painful realities.

You may completely disagree with Archer's theory or embrace it as your own. Whatever position we hold, we can affirm that the Lord yearns for *shalom*—his holistic peace—in all its fullness, whether in our nations, communities or families.

Prayer

Lord, we pray for the war-torn areas of the world and the many victims: the women who are raped, the men who are killed, the children who are orphaned. Bring peace, we pray.

ABP

The Lord lives!

The Lord lives! Praise be to my Rock! Exalted be God my Saviour! He is the God who avenges me, who subdues nations under me, who saves me from my enemies. You exalted me above my foes; from violent people you rescued me. Therefore I will praise you, Lord, among the nations; I will sing the praises of your name. He gives his king great victories; he shows unfailing love to his anointed, to David and to his descendants for ever.

As we come to the end of our journey through Psalm 18, David sings forth praise to God, his Rock, who has saved him. This psalm, like so many others, prefigures Christ our Lord, for he without sin can sing it like no other.

Some Christians pray through this psalm as they remember Jesus' trial before Pilate, his death and resurrection. They think about the cords of death entangling and confronting him (vv. 4–5). They see God's anger at the death of his beloved as he made the earth quake and shook the foundations of the earth (vv. 7–15). They praise the Lord Jesus for his purity and lack of sin (vv. 20–27). They lift their spirits in worship at the victory of Jesus over the gates of hell and death as he vanquished the enemy (vv. 32–45) and proclaim his kingdom as they join him in songs of praise to the living Lord who is their rock and saviour (vv. 46–50).

As we conclude, let us join our voices in praise to the God who loves us. Let us thank him who created us, the Lord Jesus who died to save us and the Holy Spirit who fills us with his cleansing, purifying presence. He is our rock and foundation, he shields us from our enemies and provides us with a refuge of shade and protection. We know that, though the rivers might wash over us, he reaches down from on high and takes hold of us, drawing us out of deep waters. He brings us to a spacious place where we can flourish and grow. Praise his holy and wonderful name!

Prayer

You, Lord, are perfect and you help us in all that we do. We will sing praises to your name, our rock and salvation. The Lord lives!

ABP

The meaning of the cross

For these two weeks of readings on the theme of the cross, we are looking not so much at the events of Good Friday but at its wider significance. It might seem strange to do this in September, away from Holy Week, but 14 September is Holy Cross Day, an ancient festival when Christians traditionally remember the cross and its place in their lives. Lutherans use the day for special preaching about the theology of the cross, Roman Catholics call the festival the Triumph of the Cross and Eastern Orthodox Christians call it the Exaltation of the Cross.

It is useful to have this festival outside Lent and Easter. With good reason, those seasons focus on what happened in and around Jerusalem at that time, but there can be a danger of skipping over what the cross means. This festival, though, comes at this time of year because it was on this day in September that the Church of the Holy Sepulchre in Jerusalem was dedicated in AD335. There is a legend that St Helena, the mother of Constantine (who became the Roman Emperor in 306 and later became a Christian like his mother), discovered the cross on which Jesus died in Jerusalem. She is said to have founded the Church of the Holy Sepulchre soon after-

wards, on the site of Jesus' burial. It became a place of pilgrimage, which it has continued to be over the centuries.

One of the key points about the cross is that we should never see it on its own: it must always be seen in the light of the resurrection. As Cally Hammond says in her Lent book, *Passionate Christianity* (SPCK, 2007): 'The first Christians... saw everything to do with Jesus *in the light of the resurrection*. Their faith, their understanding, their desire to reach out to others, were all conditioned by the absolute, overwhelming conviction that "God has made him both Lord and Messiah, this Jesus whom you crucified" (Acts 2:36)... They saw a simple, clear connection between the fact of the resurrection and Jesus' acceptance of death as—somehow—necessary and right.'

Most of the first of the next two weeks' Bible readings are those set by the Anglican and Roman Catholic Churches, among others, to be read on Holy Cross Day (which falls, this year, on Monday), while the second week's passages explore the meaning of the cross, as it was being worked out by Paul and the Early Church.

Rachel Boulding

19

MARK 15:22–26 (NRSV)

Redeeming an instrument of torture

Then they brought Jesus to the place called Golgotha (which means the place of a skull). And they offered him wine mixed with myrrh; but he did not take it. And they crucified him, and divided his clothes among them, casting lots to decide what each should take. It was nine o'clock in the morning when they crucified him. The inscription of the charge against him read, 'The King of the Jews.'

We begin two weeks of readings about the cross with where it all started: Jesus being crucified. Before we think about all that the cross means and does for us, it is important to start with the most obvious facts. The cross was the instrument of an extremely painful and shameful death, deliberately used by the Roman forces of occupation to oppress their subject people in the harshest and most humiliating way they could devise. On the surface, it would be hard to see any good coming out of the cross: it looks like pure defeat.

At various times, Christians have emphasised the horrific torture Jesus suffered. We can see this in gory medieval paintings and carvings, which must have rung true for people in ages when life was nasty, brutish and short. We have had a much more recent reminder of this tradition in Mel Gibson's surprisingly popular film, *The Passion of the Christ*. It used the stomach-churning techniques of horror movies to impress on the audience the pain Jesus endured.

All this seems a long way from celebrating the cross as a symbol. It might seem strange to use an instrument of torture and murder as a sign on our buildings and as a piece of jewellery. We wouldn't think of doing the same thing with a hangman's noose. Strangely, of course, it is only because of the terrible suffering that took place on it—and, most importantly, what happened later—that we can make the cross a light to illuminate our lives; it is only because of Jesus' death and resurrection that the cross is at the centre of our faith now.

Prayer

Father of all, thank you for the cross on which your Son, our Saviour, died. Help us to absorb its power and meaning into the fabric of everything we do and say and are.

RB

NUMBERS 21:5–9 (NRSV, ABRIDGED)

Trapped in restless ingratitude

The people spoke against God and against Moses, 'Why have you brought us up out of Egypt to die in the wilderness?...' Then the Lord sent poisonous serpents among the people, and they bit the people, so that many Israelites died. The people came to Moses and said, 'We have sinned by speaking against the Lord and against you; pray to the Lord to take away the serpents from us.' So Moses prayed for the people. And the Lord said to Moses, 'Make a poisonous serpent, and set it on a pole; and everyone who is bitten shall look at it and live.' So Moses made a serpent of bronze, and put it upon a pole; and whenever a serpent bit someone, that person would look at the serpent of bronze and live.

This incident is from the wanderings of the people of Israel in the desert, after they had left Egypt. It has traditionally been seen as a forerunner of the cross: the image of something malign and dangerous is transformed into something that heals; what used to lead to death now gives life. Today, the serpent entwined on a pole is a symbol of the medical profession.

God seems to be reminding the people of their utter dependence on him. They complain and are severely punished. Then they repent and are healed (though many have already died). It all seems so simple. If only we would trust God more and realise what was best for us, but we don't. We nurse our own warped sense of what we think is right. We cling on to our petty ideas of self. It's as if we trap ourselves in an ungener-ous, ungrateful attitude to our Father in heaven, who made us to love him.

Often, although we are reluctant to admit it, we cherish God's creations instead of the creator himself. As the poet George Herbert puts it by describing God as saying, humankind 'would adore my gifts instead of me'. So, Herbert continues, God gives us the restlessness that should lead us back to him, which is the only place where we can find true rest.

Reflection

Let him be rich and weary,
that at least,
If goodness lead him not,
yet weariness
May toss him to my breast.

George Herbert, 'The Pulley'
RB

JOHN 3:13–17 (NRSV)

All for love

'No one has ascended into heaven except the one who descended from heaven, the Son of Man. And just as Moses lifted up the serpent in the wilderness, so must the Son of Man be lifted up, that whoever believes in him may have eternal life. For God so loved the world that he gave his only Son, so that everyone who believes in him may not perish but may have eternal life. Indeed, God did not send the Son into the world to condemn the world, but in order that the world might be saved through him.'

Today is Holy Cross Day, and this is the Gospel passage that a number of Churches set for the festival. As noted in the Introduction, this isn't so much about the events of Good Friday as about what the cross does for us in the widest sense. So, the word 'cross' is not mentioned, but we find one of the most celebrated verses in all the Bible: John 3:16, 'For God so loved the world…'.

This is all about looking to God—like looking to the serpent in yesterday's reading—realising our dependence on him, as the Israelites had to in the wilderness, and trusting him to heal us. If we do this, we will live.

God does not want to condemn us, but to save us (v. 17). He has always loved us and his greatest wish is that we might love him and our fellow creatures. It is this love that the cross represents so powerfully. In another part of the medieval poem quoted at the end

of this reading, we are told that this love brought Jesus from heaven and 'For love thou hung on rood tree' ('rood' being an old word for 'cross'). It is not just a question of feeling sorry for Jesus' suffering but also of our responding to the love he is pouring out for each one of us.

This is demanding love, 'costing not less than everything', as T.S. Eliot put it. Jesus and his Father suffered heavily to bring us this love and forgiveness. How do we react?

Reflection and prayer

Jesu, thy love be all my thought,
Of other thing ne reck me nought;
Then have I thy will all wrought,
That havest me full dear bought.

Anonymous medieval lyric
(Note: 'reck' means 'care for')
RB

The humble and meek exalted

O praise the Lord, ye that fear him: magnify him... For he hath not despised, nor abhorred, the low estate of the poor: he hath not hid his face from him, but when he called unto him he heard him... The poor shall eat and be satisfied: they that seek after the Lord shall praise him; your heart shall live for ever. All the ends of the world shall remember themselves, and be turned unto the Lord.

This part of Psalm 22 is also set by the Churches for Holy Cross Day, to be read before the Gospel passage we had yesterday. There is a long Christian tradition of seeing this psalm as reflecting the crucifixion—particularly because of verses such as 'why hast thou forsaken me?' (v. 1) and 'They pierced my hands and my feet' (v. 16)—and it is used in churches on Maundy Thursday.

Yet the passage we have here is taken from later in the psalm and it speaks of God meeting the needs of the poor. In some ways, it seems an odd choice, but it does forge a link with the familiar New Testament ideas of Jesus coming to rescue humankind by being born as one of us. We shall follow through this theme in tomorrow's passage from Philippians.

It might seem a long way from the cross, but it is, in fact, the reason for Jesus' journey from heaven to that place of pain. He came because he loves his people, especially the poor, and he cares about their 'low estate' (v. 24). The Magnificat echoes this, drawing on God's concern for the lowly throughout the Old Testament: 'He hath put down the mighty from their seat: and hath exalted the humble and meek' (Luke 1:52, BCP).

So here is the cross as the culmination of one of the central themes of the Old Testament: God's burning desire to bring justice and honour to those who are despised by the world. He achieves this by becoming one of those lowly, rejected people—taking it to the ultimate limit of dying as a criminal.

Reflection

How can I make more links between God's love for us all and the suffering of the poor? What am I doing today to join in God's care for those whom most of us ignore?

RB

Laying aside our selves for others

Be of the same mind, having the same love, being in full accord and of one mind. Do nothing from selfish ambition or conceit, but in humility regard others as better than yourselves. Let each of you look not to your own interests, but to the interests of others. Let the same mind be in you that was in Christ Jesus, who, though he was in the form of God, did not regard equality with God as something to be exploited, but emptied himself, taking the form of a slave, being born in human likeness. And being found in human form, he humbled himself and became obedient to the point of death—even death on a cross.

This takes up the theme from yesterday's passage, in that it fills in the detail of what was needed in order to save the world and bring justice for the poor. Jesus had to empty himself—to strip himself of all his capabilities and status as the second person in the Trinity to become an ordinary man. He was to be stripped further by the Roman soldiers to become the lowest of despised men.

This takes us to the heart of what the cross is about. It shows Jesus letting go of the power, the sense of security and the knowledge of being valued—everything that the people of the world most crave—and undergoing the worst that that world can throw at him. It reminds us how far he had to go in order to bring us home.

Jesus decides to lay aside his life and abilities, so as to give us life. Richard Crashaw (1613–49) teases this out in his poem, 'On the Cross', where he describes Jesus bound on the cross, his hands nailed down, but still willing and able to choose freely to give himself for us:

Thy hands to give thou canst not lift,
Yet will thy hand still giving be;
It gives, but O, itself's the gift!
It gives though bound,
though bound 'tis free!

Reflection

Is there something that I need
to do this week to leave behind the
comforts that cocoon me from the
wants of others and reach out to
them? Is there something more
I can give to have the same
love as Christ?

RB

The painful path to glory

Therefore God also highly exalted him and gave him the name that is above every name, so that at the name of Jesus every knee should bend, in heaven and on earth and under the earth, and every tongue should confess that Jesus Christ is Lord, to the glory of God the Father.

These famous verses follow straight on from yesterday's passage and form the contrast between Jesus' death on the cross and his being exalted by God in glory. We are invited to exult in the cross of Christ—to turn the shameful instrument of death into something wonderful that we can celebrate. How on earth can we do this?

Perhaps one clue is in the route Jesus took, which the prayer below emphasises. That involves seeing suffering as an essential element on the path to glory. Pain, like death, is unavoidable, but we do have a choice about how we meet it. Obviously we should not be embittered by suffering, but our choice concerns whether or not we should expect it in the first place.

Some of us (especially in Western societies) seem surprised by any troubles we meet, as if we have a bizarre right to be treated better than anyone else. We know, deep down, that being a Christian does not protect us from suffering, but we sometimes behave as if we have earned the right to float above

it. Earlier generations were more in touch with physical hardship and death in the midst of life than we are today. Because of that, many of them had a stronger sense of their dependence on God. We, in contrast, have more to be thankful for, because of technological and medical advances, but seem to find it harder to be grateful to God than did people in days gone by.

The Collect (the special prayer that collects together themes) for Holy Cross Day (below) brings together pain and exaltation and weaves them into the wholeness that Christ offers us. On the one hand, there is humiliation, suffering and death; on the other, life, reconciliation with God and glory.

Prayer

Almighty God, who in the passion of your blessed Son, made an instrument of painful death to be for us the means of life and peace: grant us so to glory in the cross of Christ that we may gladly suffer for his sake.

Common Worship
RB

25

Lose your life, for God's sake

Then said Jesus unto his disciples, If any man will come after me, let him deny himself, and take up his cross, and follow me. For whosoever will save his life shall lose it: and whosoever will lose his life for my sake shall find it. For what is a man profited, if he shall gain the whole world, and lose his own soul? or what shall a man give in exchange for his soul? For the Son of man shall come in the glory of his Father with his angels; and then he shall reward every man according to his works.

The rest of the Bible passages for these readings on the theme of the cross move beyond those set for Holy Cross Day to look at other ideas associated with it. In the order in which they appear in the New Testament, these actually start well before the crucifixion itself. One of the main threads is that of taking up our own cross of self-denial for the sake of Christ.

This develops what we read yesterday in Philippians, about suffering and glory being inextricably bound together, and moves it into a different area—that of deliberately choosing to leave behind caring for ourselves in order to follow Jesus. The image is one of our willingly shouldering a burden in order to imitate Christ and draw closer to him. We would gain a sense of focusing so much on him that we forget about our own needs, troubles and desires.

Following on from Sunday's reading, in connection with the Israelites' clinging on to their sinful ways in the wilderness instead of trusting God, this is another way to describe the universal tendency to cherish our own delights. Many of us do something horribly similar. We would rather nurse our selfishness than open ourselves up to love and allow God and other people in: 'Men loved darkness rather than light, because their deeds were evil' (John 3:19).

Reflection

We need a wider perspective and an eternal timeframe. To return to the words of Richard Crashaw:

The world's light shines;
shine as it will,
The world will love
its darkness still:
I doubt though
when the world's in Hell,
It will not love its darkness
half so well.

RB

The cost of discipleship

[Jesus] said to [the crowd], 'Whoever comes to me and does not hate father and mother, wife and children, brothers and sisters, yes, and even life itself, cannot be my disciple. Whoever does not carry the cross and follow me cannot be my disciple. For which of you, intending to build a tower, does not first sit down and estimate the cost, to see whether he has enough to complete it? Otherwise, when he has laid a foundation and is not able to finish, all who see it will begin to ridicule him.'

Jesus is saying more than just 'Focus on me and forget yourself.' He is asking us to weigh up whether or not we are prepared for the cost of taking up our cross. He knows that if we do not do this, we will fall away. We need to take our discipleship seriously enough that we do not get swept up in our new enthusiasm like a passing fad that fades as quickly as it came.

The cross is the ultimate symbol of this. It means that we can die to whatever separates us from God. So, we should consider carefully whether or not we are prepared to take up this work of love, which may involve turning away from those closest to us and from life itself (v. 26).

Ought we really to neglect our responsibilities for God's sake, though? Jesus uses deliberately exaggerated language ('hate' is more of a figure of speech for 'loves... more than', which is how this is worded in the equivalent passage in Matthew 10:37). Jesus does not suggest abandoning any obligations to them, but, rather, perhaps means that we should not rely on them completely for our ultimate happiness. He might well be critical of the modern tendency to idealise family life, weighing it down with the intolerable burden of being the source of our fulfilment. Many of us are guilty of worshipping this idol rather than God.

We must be wholeheartedly for God, responding to the love shown on the cross with an unstinting love of our own.

Reflection

But just the way that thou didst me
I do love and I will love thee;
What must I love thee,
Lord, for then?
For being my king and God. Amen

Gerard Manley Hopkins,
'O Deus Ego Amo Te'
RB

1 CORINTHIANS 1:18, 22–25 (NRSV)

The world doesn't get it

For the message about the cross is foolishness to those who are perishing, but to us who are being saved it is the power of God... Jews demand signs and Greeks desire wisdom, but we proclaim Christ crucified, a stumbling block to Jews and foolishness to Gentiles, but to those who are the called, both Jews and Greeks, Christ the power of God and the wisdom of God. For God's foolishness is wiser than human wisdom, and God's weakness is stronger than human strength.

Despite being an instrument of oppression and judicial murder, the cross has been transformed into something that demonstrates the power and wisdom of God. No wonder most people just don't understand it.

As with the Beatitudes and the rest of the Sermon on the Mount, God turns the wisdom of the world on its head: 'Blessed are those who mourn', 'Love your enemies and pray for those who persecute you' (see Matthew 5:4, 44). It's the opposite of normal common sense, but then God's wisdom is so utterly different that it gets to the heart of life in a much deeper way. He exposes our foolish wickedness.

God redeems us, buying back what was and really is his own by thoroughly undermining the wrongdoing that can drive a wedge between him and us. Jesus' actions on the cross show us a better way to respond to the wickedness around us. Jesus meets the cruelty of his torturers with kindness. He knows that they do not realise what they are doing. His pure heart beats with the same pulse as his Father's.

God's kingdom is ordered differently from the world, so we need each day to realign ourselves with his values. The world does not understand them and so is the ultimate loser. People abandon their souls as they struggle to reach the top, only to find that their victories are hollow.

Prayer

Lift up our minds to the pure, bright serene atmosphere of thy presence; that we may breathe freely, there repose in thy love, there be at rest from ourselves and from all things that weary us: and thence return, arrayed in thy peace, to do and to bear whatsoever shall best please thee, O blessed Lord.

E.B. Pusey (1800–1882)
RB

Reconciled through the cross

For in him all the fullness of God was pleased to dwell, and through him God was pleased to reconcile to himself all things, whether on earth or in heaven, by making peace through the blood of his cross. And you who were once estranged and hostile in mind, doing evil deeds, he has now reconciled in his fleshly body through death, so as to present you holy and blameless and irreproachable before him.

At last, we reach what will be one of the most familiar ideas relating to the cross—that what Jesus did there brought together God and human beings. We, his creatures, had wandered away from our loving creator through sin, but Christ on the cross brought us back home. Most of us know the old drawing of a chasm, with God on one side, humankind on the other and the cross forming a bridge between the two.

Over the centuries, Christians have put forward a number of different ideas about exactly how this works—the theories of the atonement. One of the commonest of these is that Jesus took upon himself the punishment for humans' sins, and died because someone had to pay the price for such wickedness. This is so familiar that many Christians haven't really heard of any other possible approaches, but other Christians see it differently.

They are unhappy about the possible implication that God the Father is so angry about sin that he needs to punish people, including his own son. They prefer to talk about Jesus' willing sacrifice, bringing us all closer to God, in the same way that giving up something for the sake of others can transform a situation.

This approach sees the cross and resurrection as being inextricably linked—that is, Jesus represents us all so that we can join in his death to sin as well as his resurrection. We share in this sacrifice every time we celebrate Holy Communion, recalling his death and rising again.

Reflection

Almighty God, our heavenly Father, who of thy tender mercy didst give thine only Son Jesus Christ to suffer death upon the cross for our redemption; who made there (by his one oblation of himself once offered) a full, perfect, and sufficient sacrifice, oblation, and satisfaction, for the sins of the whole world…

Holy Communion service (BCP)

RB

Nail in the coffin

When you were buried with him in baptism, you were also raised with him through faith in the power of God, who raised him from the dead. And when you were dead in trespasses and the uncircumcision of your flesh, God made you alive together with him, when he forgave us all our trespasses, erasing the record that stood against us with its legal demands. He set this aside, nailing it to the cross.

Whatever way we explain it, Christians know that Christ died for our sins on the cross. One vivid way to express this is the idea here of Paul's of nailing our sins to the cross. In this way we can put them to death so that they can no longer have power over us. Paul links this to baptism and the crucial Christian idea that some things—good as well as bad—have to die completely before they can be raised to new life. As Jesus himself said, 'unless a grain of wheat falls into the earth and dies, it remains just a single grain; but if it dies, it bears much fruit' (John 12:24). Sin desensitises us as, when we know we are doing wrong, we suppress our better instincts, which would lead us to a covenant with God (hence 'uncircumcision of your flesh').

The idea of dumping our unpleasant aspects, fixing them to the cross, is hugely appealing, but what about the parts that we sneakily think are not so bad? Those talents and attitudes in which we take a self-satisfied pride, fancying ourselves a little better than the next person? Are we ever content to give ourselves over to God and let him decide?

We have to die fully with Christ, not just partially. We cannot hold back those parts of ourselves that we think we can do all right with. That is surely what the cross means—complete death to the old self (see also Galatians 6:14–15).

Prayer

I am no longer my own but yours. Put me to what you will, rank me with whom you will; put me to doing, put me to suffering… let me have all things, let me have nothing: I freely and wholeheartedly yield all things to your pleasure and disposal.

From the Methodist Covenant Service
RB

'Burn off my rusts'

Christ also suffered for you, leaving you an example... 'He committed no sin, and no deceit was found in his mouth.' When he was abused, he did not return abuse; when he suffered, he did not threaten; but he entrusted himself to the one who judges justly. He himself bore our sins in his body on the cross, so that, free from sins, we might live for righteousness; by his wounds you have been healed. For you were going astray like sheep, but now you have returned to the shepherd and guardian of your souls.

This is the next stage in the cosmic significance of the cross. Christ has taken the initiative and is suffering for us in order to heal us. As we saw yesterday, we need to submit ourselves fully to this process and join in with his actions. This is part of what we do at Communion services, re-enacting his sacrifice. It is amazing that we can share actively in this in our worship.

These steps towards healing can be painful. If we are wholeheartedly subjecting ourselves to his loving gaze, we should start to see ourselves as he does—the best as well as the worst. It's always a useful exercise to try to see situations and our part in them from another person's point of view—'some Pow'r the giftie gie us/ To see oursels as others see us', as Robert Burns put it. It's even more useful to imagine what God might think of it all. We are made in his image, so the pattern is there for us to follow.

The thoroughly worthwhile question 'What would Jesus do?' has become almost a cliché, a motto for bracelets and ballpoint pens. All the same, it hints at a great truth: that God can guide us through anything that might be thrown at us. We can 'live for righteousness' in each circumstance. So, when we are healed and back at home in God, we will be able to face our troubles in his strength, by his grace.

Reflection

O think me worth thine anger,
punish me,
Burn off my rusts and my deformity,
Restore thine Image so much,
by thy grace,
That thou may'st know me,
and I'll turn my face.

John Donne, 'Good Friday, 1613,
Riding Westward'
RB

Raised to life with God

But if we have died with Christ, we believe that we will also live with him. We know that Christ, being raised from the dead, will never die again; death no longer has dominion over him. The death he died, he died to sin, once for all; but the life he lives, he lives to God. So you also must consider yourselves dead to sin and alive to God in Christ Jesus.

This celebrated passage further unpacks the way that the cross has to be seen in the light of the resurrection. Jesus has done his work on the cross, once for all time and all people, so that we can be released from the power of sin and death.

This is why many Christians prefer to display an empty cross. Jesus is no longer there, for he has risen. Other Christians, while fully realising this, want to emphasise what Jesus died on the cross, undergoing that pain for us. They prefer a crucifix showing a figure of Christ suffering, but reaching out to us in love. Both these aspects of his life are true and we need to reflect on both of them at different times.

Whichever way we think about the precise workings of this, we can see that Jesus' sufferings on the cross mean that God knows from the inside the worst of what it is like to be human. It also means that, in his turn, Jesus can raise us from misery, towards his own god-liness. As the Collect (the special prayer for that day) for the first Sunday of Christmas puts it, 'as he came to share in our humanity, so we may share the life of his divinity' (*Common Worship*).

We are raised with him—not just away from sin and death, but further, towards God. The Orthodox Church has made more of this truth than we have in the West. Irenaeus (c.125–202), a Greek who was Bishop of Lyons in France, wrote, 'God has become what we are, so that we might become what God is.'

Reflection

'As we keep this feast [of the cross], we are lifted up with the crucified Christ, leaving behind us earth and sin, so that we may gain the things above.'

Andrew of Crete (c.660–740), a sermon on the exaltation of the holy cross

RB

New every morning is the love

Wherefore seeing we also are compassed about with so great a cloud of witnesses, let us lay aside every weight, and the sin which doth so easily beset us, and let us run with patience the race that is set before us, looking unto Jesus the author and finisher of our faith; who for the joy that was set before him endured the cross, despising the shame, and is set down at the right hand of the throne of God.

We don't allow ourselves much triumph. It can so easily turn into boasting and, for those of us who are British, it lacks the self-deprecating humour that we like to think is our natural mode. We should triumph in the victory of the cross, though. It was hard-won and that battle was fought specially for us.

An Anglo-Saxon poem offers an approach that can encourage an appropriate sense of triumph. Written anonymously some time between the seventh and tenth centuries, 'The Dream of the Rood' tells of a vision of the cross, now honoured and covered in jewels. It imagines the cross itself speaking about Jesus, seeing him as a triumphant warrior, not a victim—truly 'the author and finisher of our faith' (v. 2): 'The young hero—who was God Almighty—stripped himself, resolute and strong; he mounted the gallows, brave before the crowd: he wished to redeem mankind.'

How can we recover this sense of confidence in our everyday lives? We can approach the truths of our triumphant faith in ways that give it new life. One way that I have found helpful is to do so through poems, such as those that I have quoted in these notes. We can also try to be more attentive in our prayer lives to what Jesus did on the cross and our loving response. Could we carve out a little more time to recall this each day?

I have read purely secular magazine articles that suggest one of the ways to boost inner contentment is to remember gratefully at the end of each day the things that have gone well. Surely we can do better than this pale version of true contentment, starved as it is of the love of God, the warm thankfulness we can all feel for our Father and creator.

Reflection

What can I do today to help myself realise how amazing divine love is?

RB

John 1:1—3:21

Imagine in your mind's eye the most beautiful sunrise that you have ever seen. Notice how the pure, clear rays pour themselves out over the darkness of the waiting earth, still night-bound and in shadow. No words can capture the splendour of the Prologue to John's Gospel, but maybe such an image might come close.

The sun is rising on a dark and bewildered world. A spiritual sunrise announces new beginnings, it heralds a new day, a turning point in time and history. It dawns in a blaze of light that will forever banish the darkness. It points to an entirely new future, yet, paradoxically, it was always there, from before the beginning of time and space, always bringing forth everything that exists. This light is the source of all that we are and John leads us into a journey of discovery about what that light means for us, what it asks of us and how it leads us towards our destiny as the sons and daughters of God—if we choose to embrace it.

During the next two weeks, we will take the first steps on the journey that God invites us to make, through the words of John. We will find that paradox will be our companion along the way. There are some truths that can perhaps only be expressed in terms that seem contradictory to our logical minds. The mystics have always known that deep paradoxes lie at the heart of revealed truth.

We learn, for example, that the one we seek is not easily found. Though present in every moment, he is at the same time 'one we do not know'. He is hidden in the wilderness of our experience. He comes from a place where we think nothing good could come from. He asks for our emptiness, not our fullness, in which to work his transforming miracles. He deconstructs much of what we thought we had got together in order to rebuild what shall come. He brings us to new birth—uniquely, unpredictably, all-powerfully.

It all begins with love. God's unconditional love is the destiny towards which we strive. Jesus himself invites us to discover that love and not by following a set of rules but by following a person— the one who calls each one of us to 'come and see'.

Margaret Silf

The light of faith

In the beginning was the Word, and the Word was with God, and the Word was God. He was in the beginning with God. All things came into being through him, and without him not one thing came into being. What has come into being in him was life, and the life was the light of all people. The light shines in the darkness, and the darkness did not overcome it. There was a man sent from God, whose name was John. He came as a witness to testify to the light, so that all might believe through him. He himself was not the light, but he came to testify to the light. The true light, which enlightens everyone, was coming into the world.

When we contemplate eternity, we very soon realise that we are way out of our depth. 'The beginning' is completely out of range of the human mind, just as surely as our eternal destiny is beyond our understanding. Yet here the evangelist assures us that the Word, the logos, the deep wisdom of all that is, has been with God from the beginning. Creation, and our own part in it, are held for ever in this wisdom, this light, this love.

In a painting by Rembrandt, the artist depicts John the Baptist addressing a gathering of people on a rocky hillside. The surrounding world is shown swathed in darkness and the skies obscured by cloud. Most of the people are also crouching in the darkness, but a pool of light falls around the Baptist himself and those closest to him. That pool of light is a token of the eternal light of which

John is speaking, not the light itself but a token of the light that is coming into the world. It represents a light that shines in the heart of the one who trusts God.

So it is that we begin our journey with John, with an invitation to come out of the shadows, to trust the pool of light that John sheds on the way ahead and follow where it points.

Reflection

In our darkest moments, dare we trust the pool of light that our faith reveals? Dare we step out into it and let it point us towards the ocean of God's eternal light?

MS

Out of the shadows

He was in the world, and the world came into being through him; yet the world did not know him. He came to what was his own, and his own people did not accept him. But to all who received him, who believed in his name, he gave power to become children of God, who were born, not of blood or of the will of the flesh or of the will of man, but of God.

The Greek philosopher Plato used a striking image to try to help his students understand the difference between temporal and eternal reality. He suggested that we are like people crouching inside a cave with our backs to the sun that is beaming down outside. In that world beyond the cave, wonderful things are happening and the fullness of life is unfolding, but we cave-dwellers see only the shadows of ourselves cast on the cave wall.

As the shadows are all that we see, we are convinced our shadow-world is the whole reality. If given the opportunity we will argue our case—the case for a false reality—very forcibly and we may even do violence to anyone who suggests that we are missing the point. This is exactly what John warns will happen to Jesus—the one who knows the light and brings it right into the cave.

For those who dare to risk leaving the cave of their own darkness to walk out into the light, a very new reality reveals itself. To them, a wholly transformed way of living, seeing, being, opens up, but they will not be accepted by the ones who remain doggedly inside the cave, gazing at the shadows.

In Jesus, John tells us, the source of everything we are is revealed—among us, in a human form that we can follow and relate to, calling us to become the sons and daughters of God. It's a pretty awesome thought, but here it is in black and white. We are being transformed into the children of God, through the power of the one who calls us out of the cave and into the light.

Reflection

If I turn my back on the light,
I will see only my own shadow.
'Conversion' asks me only
to 'turn round'.

MS

Earthing the power

And the Word became flesh and lived among us, and we have seen his glory, the glory as of a father's only son, full of grace and truth. (John testified to him and cried out, 'This was he of whom I said, "He who comes after me ranks ahead of me because he was before me."')

We all know the power of the sun that sustains our physical life on earth, but we also know that we can't plug our kettles straight into the sun. The energy we need for life first has to be 'earthed', grounded, brought down to our level so that we may access it in safety. We are also warned never to look straight into the sun because it might blind us. We can only look on the sun's light indirectly or through the filter of protective lenses.

So, too, we cannot gaze on God, nor can we access the power of God directly as it would totally overwhelm us. We need it to be earthed and grounded. It is Jesus who brings God's immense and immeasurable power down to earth, so that it might flow through our own lives, healing us, transforming us, but not burning us up.

When I was a child, I remember singing the words of a familiar hymn: 'Immortal, invisible, God only wise, in light inaccessible hid from our eyes.' At the time I hadn't a clue what those words might mean. One line, though, took root in my imagination at a deeper level than my mind could understand: ''Tis only the splendour of light hideth thee.'

We know that if we go out into a brilliant light, we are, at least temporarily, blinded. Today, John tells us that the God whom we seek in vain in our own darkness is actually at the heart of all light, but that light will be earthed and grounded in the one who invites us into God's undying love. When he comes, we are not blinded, but our 'sight' is transformed into 'insight'.

Reflection

Jesus comes to live among us, journey with us, lead us towards our eternal destiny. He shows us what the glory of God actually looks like and invites us to bathe in its radiance.

MS

A voice in the wilderness

From his fullness we have all received, grace upon grace. The law indeed was given through Moses; grace and truth came through Jesus Christ. No one has ever seen God. It is God the only Son, who is close to the Father's heart, who has made him known. This is the testimony given by John when the Jews sent priests and Levites from Jerusalem to ask him, 'Who are you?' He confessed and did not deny it, but confessed, 'I am not the Messiah.' And they asked him, 'What then? Are you Elijah?' He said, 'I am not.' 'Are you the prophet?' He answered, 'No.' Then they said to him, 'Who are you? Let us have an answer for those who sent us. What do you say about yourself?' He said, 'I am the voice of one crying out in the wilderness, "Make straight the way of the Lord,"' as the prophet Isaiah said.

This is going to be a journey that begins with the law, as given through Moses, and leads to Love, as revealed in the one 'who is close to the Father's heart'. We, like John's followers, know what the law has to say, but what does Love have to say of itself? How does Love describe itself? Who is this man who baptises people in the Jordan in preparation for the coming of the one who embodies God's love in human form?

John the Baptist describes himself as 'the voice of one crying out in the wilderness'. In our world today, it can very easily feel that the fragile expression of love is just such a faint cry in a wilderness of violence, deception and desolation. Can this faint cry really be effective? Can it make a straight path where there is so much convolution and confusion? How do we ourselves join our voices to that of the one crying in the wilderness?

I suggest that we do so every time we choose, in however small a way, the more loving response or reaction in any given situation.

Reflection

Each time I ask: 'What is the more Christ-like thing to do next?' I am helping to make straight the way of the Lord. May I have the humility to ask the question and the courage to live the answer.

MS

The one we do not know

Now they had been sent from the Pharisees. They asked him, 'Why then are you baptising if you are neither the Messiah, nor Elijah, nor the prophet?' John answered them, 'I baptise with water. Among you stands one whom you do not know, the one who is coming after me; I am not worthy to untie the thong of his sandal.' This took place in Bethany across the Jordan where John was baptising.

There was once a church in a small town. Many people worshipped there, and it started off as a vibrant and caring community in which the people of the neighbourhood could see the power of the risen Christ. Over the years, however, things started to slide downhill. Some of the church members fell into serious dispute with one another. Gradually the rot spread. The atmosphere in the church became toxic. There was back-biting among the people and spiteful comments and underhand dealings. The pastor became deeply disturbed about the bad state of the church and sought the advice of a local hermit who was known to be wise and compassionate.

The advice of the wise mentor was this: 'Start a rumour among the people that the Messiah is among them.' Amazed at this advice, the pastor nevertheless went back to his people and did as he had been advised. Gradually the story went the rounds—'the Messiah is among us!' Who could

it be? Who was this blessed one who stood among them whom they did not know?

A miracle came in the wake of the rumour. The people began to see each other with new eyes. They began to treat each other with respect. They even began to love one another. After all, any one of them could be the Messiah in disguise!

The Messiah still moves among us, as one we do not know. He asks us to honour and love him in everyone we meet, most especially the unlovely and the unlovable. His presence among us and within us is the catalyst for transformation and our recognition of that presence in each other is the response he asks of us.

Reflection

If you knew that the next person you meet might be the Messiah, how might that transform your attitude and how might it change the world?

MS

39

Following the one who was always there

The next day [John] saw Jesus coming towards him and declared, 'Here is the Lamb of God who takes away the sin of the world! This is he of whom I said, "After me comes a man who ranks ahead of me because he was before me." I myself did not know him; but I came baptizing with water for this reason, that he might be revealed to Israel.' And John testified, 'I saw the Spirit descending from heaven like a dove, and it remained on him. I myself did not know him, but the one who sent me to baptize with water said to me, "He on whom you see the Spirit descend and remain is the one who baptizes with the Holy Spirit." And I myself have seen and have testified that this is the Son of God.'

We hear today that John sees Jesus coming *towards* him and yet, in the next breath, he tells us that the promised one is coming after him, but is ahead of him. Just a turn of phrase, perhaps, but isn't it also a reflection of something of our own experience of God? We spend so much of our lives striving to move towards God and, in those moments of truth, when we become more deeply aware of God's presence, we find that, actually, God has the whole time been coming towards *us*.

The spiritual journey is full of paradoxes and so the mystery of God is perhaps best expressed in human terms in ways that strike us as contradictory. Here, on the banks of the Jordan, the one who brings the power to baptise us with the very Spirit of God humbly submits to the human ritual of baptism with water, at John's hands. Perhaps for us, too, the religious traditions in which our own spiritual journeys are rooted invite us to engage with the sacred rituals that are passed down to us through the generations. The time comes, though, sometimes so quietly that we almost miss it, when we realise God's Spirit is indeed coming towards us and has always been there, one step ahead of us, hovering over our hearts, inviting us forwards.

Reflection

May we faithfully follow the one who was always there before us and leads us beyond ourselves.

MS

Come and see

The next day John again was standing with two of his disciples, and as he watched Jesus walk by, he exclaimed, 'Look, here is the Lamb of God!' The two disciples heard him say this, and they followed Jesus. When Jesus turned and saw them following, he said to them, 'What are you looking for?' They said to him, 'Rabbi' (which translated means Teacher), 'where are you staying?' He said to them, 'Come and see.' They came and saw where he was staying, and they remained with him that day. It was about four o'clock in the afternoon. One of the two who heard John speak and followed him was Andrew, Simon Peter's brother. He first found his brother Simon and said to him, 'We have found the Messiah' (which is translated Anointed). He brought Simon to Jesus, who looked at him and said, 'You are Simon son of John. You are to be called Cephas' (which is translated Peter).

I will never forget one summer afternoon. I was in town, shopping. It was about four o'clock. I stopped to speak to a homeless person, begging in the street. I fetched him something to eat from the local cafe and we had a conversation. It was no big deal for me. We were there in broad daylight, safe among hundreds of busy shoppers. I listened as he told me something of his story.

Then, without thinking of the implications of what I was saying, I found myself asking, 'Where do you stay? Where do you sleep?' His answer came instantly and cut through me like a knife: 'Come and see.'

He led me down to the basement of the multi-storey car park. My heart was thumping. This was definitely *not* comfortable. He showed me a filthy mattress in a dark corner. My common sense knew that it was stupidly dangerous to be down here and yet, in that moment, in those words, I knew that I had also met Jesus, down there in the squalor.

Reflection

When Jesus says, 'Come and see', there is no knowing where the journey may lead. Only when we follow will we discover for ourselves the answer to his question: 'What are you looking for?' Perhaps the answer is: 'You!'

MS

True colours

The next day Jesus decided to go to Galilee. He found Philip and said to him, 'Follow me.' Now Philip was from Bethsaida, the city of Andrew and Peter. Philip found Nathanael and said to him, 'We have found him about whom Moses in the law and also the prophets wrote, Jesus son of Joseph from Nazareth.' Nathanael said to him, 'Can anything good come out of Nazareth?' Philip said to him, 'Come and see.' When Jesus saw Nathanael coming towards him, he said of him, 'Here is truly an Israelite in whom there is no deceit!' Nathanael asked him, 'Where did you get to know me?' Jesus answered, 'I saw you under the fig tree before Philip called you.' Nathanael replied, 'Rabbi, you are the Son of God! You are the King of Israel!' Jesus answered, 'Do you believe because I told you that I saw you under the fig tree? You will see greater things than these.' And he said to him, 'Very truly, I tell you, you will see heaven opened and the angels of God ascending and descending upon the Son of Man.'

I love to imagine Nathanael sitting there under the fig tree, possibly engaged in deep conversation or maybe just enjoying a well-earned rest. Then along comes Philip, with the amazing news that they have met Jesus, the promised one, foretold by the prophets long ago. Nathanael dismisses the thought: what good could ever come out of a place like Nazareth? Then we hear Philip's invitation, echoing the invitation of Jesus that we followed yesterday: 'Come and see'.

How often do we dismiss people because their faces don't fit or they come from the wrong neighbourhood or speak with the wrong accent? If we take the trouble to get to know them, though, we discover a very different story. Our superficial judgments are shown up for what they are. Nathanael has the grace to allow himself to be taken beyond his prejudice and, when he does, he meets the one who immediately sees the real person underneath the superficial appearance, the one who knows him in his true colours.

Reflection

We would never throw away a gift just because we didn't like the colour or pattern of the wrapping paper. Why do we so easily dismiss other human beings on such a flimsy basis?

MS

Sunday 4 October
John 2:1–7 (NRSV)

Empty vessels

On the third day there was a wedding in Cana of Galilee, and the mother of Jesus was there. Jesus and his disciples had also been invited to the wedding. When the wine gave out, the mother of Jesus said to him, 'They have no wine.' And Jesus said to her, 'Woman, what concern is that to you and to me? My hour has not yet come.' His mother said to the servants, 'Do whatever he tells you.' Now standing there were six stone water jars for the Jewish rites of purification, each holding twenty or thirty gallons. Jesus said to them, 'Fill the jars with water.' And they filled them up to the brim.

Most of us are not likely to find ourselves at a wedding where the wine runs out. If we did, we would, rightly, think that it wasn't our problem. In one way, it isn't Jesus' problem either, as he points out to his mother. They are simply guests there and the catering arrangements are not their responsibility. In a deeper sense, though, this incident is very much about what Jesus has come to do. In these few verses, a pattern becomes visible and says what Jesus is about, how he acts, how he has come to bring transformation.

It begins with need: 'They have no wine.' God's actions in our own lives usually begin in the same way. We turn to him in our need. We acknowledge that we can't make it on our own. We recognise our own helplessness.

Then comes the call to obedience, for us to surrender ourselves, without question or argument, to one who is wiser than we: 'Do whatever he tells you.' This isn't blind obedience, this is trust. It is about knowing that we cannot help ourselves and acknowledging our need of God in the situations in which we find ourselves.

Then comes the filling up, but, before the jars can be filled up, they must first be empty. Our emptiness is the raw material of transformation. It is all God needs to work his miracles in our lives.

Reflection
God chooses emptiness to reveal himself—an empty womb, an empty tomb, an empty life. May we resist the temptation to fill up our inner emptiness with anything less than God.

MS

Poured out

[Jesus] said to them, 'Now draw some out, and take it to the chief steward.' So they took it. When the steward tasted the water that had become wine, and did not know where it had come from (though the servants who had drawn the water knew), the steward called the bridegroom and said to him, 'Everyone serves the good wine first, and then the inferior wine after the guests have become drunk. But you have kept the good wine until now.' Jesus did this, the first of his signs, in Cana of Galilee, and revealed his glory; and his disciples believed in him. After this he went down to Capernaum with his mother, his brothers, and his disciples; and they remained there a few days.

The miracle happens silently, secretly, in the hidden depths of the stone water jars. Transformation is like that. As a butterfly shapes itself silently in the chrysalis, as a child is formed silently in the womb, so transformation happens in ways that we cannot see, control or understand.

Now we, and maybe those wedding guests who were privy to the wine crisis, can see that this is about so much more than wine. What Jesus has done to transform the water into wine is a sign of how God is longing to transform the people we think we are into the people God has created us to be. Yet that transformation still needs one more step before the miracle is manifest.

The wine must be poured out. If it is not poured out, it might as well still be water. Jesus knows this, too, and invites the servants to draw it out and take it to the chief steward for tasting. When God touches our lives, there is also a call for us to be poured out, for each other. Only then will it be apparent whether our hearts have been transformed or we are still living for ourselves alone.

It's never too late for this to happen. When God has touched a human heart, that person becomes living wine for others. God often saves the best until last, so, just when we think that we are past all possibility of change, the greatest change may be just about to happen.

Reflection
Dare we allow ourselves to be poured out?

MS

JOHN 2:13–17 (NRSV)

Deconstruction

The Passover of the Jews was near, and Jesus went up to Jerusalem. In the temple he found people selling cattle, sheep, and doves, and the money changers seated at their tables. Making a whip of cords, he drove all of them out of the temple, both the sheep and the cattle. He also poured out the coins of the money changers and overturned their tables. He told those who were selling the doves, 'Take these things out of here! Stop making my Father's house a marketplace!' His disciples remembered that it was written, 'Zeal for your house will consume me.'

Here we have a very different and dramatic scene. Yesterday we were present at a moment of completely unexpected creativity on Jesus' part—the transformation of water into wine and everything that this signifies for both our own lives and the life of the world. Today we witness a scene of apparent destruction as Jesus storms into the temple, driving out those who are, as he puts it, turning the temple into a marketplace and tipping over their tables and flinging their coins around.

It looks terrifying, leaving us wondering what he would make of the gift shops in our own churches and cathedrals. Perhaps, though, his anger has deeper roots than this.

At Cana we saw how Jesus first had to have emptiness before he could bring about a rich fullness, but his divine purpose was ultimately to transform, to bring a greater measure of life. Now, in the temple, what we observe is also to do with bringing a greater fullness to humanity. Here, too, something has to be emptied out before it can be filled with what is greater. Jesus first has to deconstruct everything that is holding us back, pulling us down. In this case it is the dominating and exploitative market forces that can so easily take over our hearts, even in the holiest of places, and the corruption of what should be held in sacred trust.

Only when he has deconstructed all that is out of order can he build up that which makes us properly fully human: community, right relationship, justice and love.

Reflection

Sometimes God's creative love demands the breaking down of whatever blocks or obscures it. What blocks is Jesus asking to overturn and break down in your heart?

MS

Breaking down, building up

The Jews then said to him, 'What sign can you show us for doing this?' Jesus answered them, 'Destroy this temple, and in three days I will raise it up.' The Jews then said, 'This temple has been under construction for forty-six years, and will you raise it up in three days?' But he was speaking of the temple of his body. After he was raised from the dead, his disciples remembered that he had said this; and they believed the scripture and the word that Jesus had spoken. When he was in Jerusalem during the Passover festival, many believed in his name because they saw the signs that he was doing. But Jesus on his part would not entrust himself to them, because he knew all people and needed no one to testify about anyone; for he himself knew what was in everyone.

We can perhaps imagine the questions and challenges: 'What on earth do you think you are doing? You'd better have a good reason for causing this mayhem.' Jesus is who he is, though. He doesn't need to justify himself to anyone and he knows it. Even more, he knows what lies in the hearts of his challengers. He doesn't need a reference. He knows that people will believe in him only when their hearts are touched by his.

Even so, he gives them a 'sign' in his enigmatic prophecy that, if the temple is destroyed, he will build it up again in three days. His listeners, predictably, get stuck at the literal level of this prophecy. They have been building the temple for 46 years, so how can a single man rebuild it in just three days?

Jesus is talking about more than a temple here, however, just as at Cana he was dealing with more than just wine. He knows that a breaking down will necessarily precede the building up that he has come to do. Indeed, he himself will be apparently destroyed, before he rises to the complete fullness of life. Similarly, many of our human ways of doing things have to be broken before they can be healed.

Reflection

Breaking down, building up, breaking through: we see here the pattern of Jesus' entire ministry. What does it mean in our own lives?

MS

Born again

Now there was a Pharisee named Nicodemus, a leader of the Jews. He came to Jesus by night and said to him, 'Rabbi, we know that you are a teacher who has come from God; for no one can do these signs that you do apart from the presence of God.' Jesus answered him, 'Very truly, I tell you, no one can see the kingdom of God without being born from above.' Nicodemus said to him, 'How can anyone be born after having grown old? Can one enter a second time into the mother's womb and be born?' Jesus answered, 'Very truly, I tell you, no one can enter the kingdom of God without being born of water and Spirit. What is born of the flesh is flesh, and what is born of the Spirit is spirit. Do not be astonished that I said to you, "You must be born from above."'

Nicodemus is clearly a man who takes things literally. He asks how can a full-grown person enter into the small space of their mother's womb again after he or she has been born? Jesus, however, makes it clear that, as always, he is addressing questions that lie deeper than the obvious. In our own times, although we are not likely to take Jesus' metaphor of rebirth literally, we can still get our minds fixed on a particular way in which that rebirth reveals itself.

Many Christians have a definite pattern of spiritual rebirth in mind when they speak of being 'born again', but, in fact, no two spiritual births are the same, just as no two physical births are the same. Each of us will experience the midwifery of God in a unique way as he draws us forth into a new dimension of our spiritual life. For some that touch will be dramatic and they will always remember the date and time and place it happened. For others it will be so gentle and gradual that they would be hard-pressed to describe it. For some it is a once-in-a-lifetime event. For others it recurs in different ways, according to their need for it.

Reflection

What does it mean to you, to be 'born again'? Have you been able to listen to other people as they share their, perhaps rather different, experiences?

MS

The wind of the Spirit

'The wind blows where it chooses, and you hear the sound of it, but you do not know where it comes from or where it goes. So it is with everyone who is born of the Spirit.' Nicodemus said to him, 'How can these things be?' Jesus answered him, 'Are you a teacher of Israel, and yet you do not understand these things? Very truly, I tell you, we speak of what we know and testify to what we have seen; yet you do not receive our testimony. If I have told you about earthly things and you do not believe, how can you believe if I tell you about heavenly things? No one has ascended into heaven except the one who descended from heaven, the Son of Man. And just as Moses lifted up the serpent in the wilderness, so must the Son of Man be lifted up, that whoever believes in him may have eternal life.'

Spiritual birth is not a process that follows a predictable pattern. As we saw yesterday, it is an experience that is unique for every individual. Like the wind, God's workings take their own directions and are not ours to control. He moves where he will, with whatever strength he will and in whatever direction he will.

The wind is an unseen reality. We can't see it but we can see its effects! We can see how it carries seeds to a new place of germination and growth. We can see how it sweeps away the debris of old growth and dead wood. We can feel it on our skin and see the branches sway in its power.

So it is, too, with the Holy Spirit. We know the power of the Spirit by the effects the Spirit has. When our hearts have been quickened into life by the Spirit, our lives will bear the fruits of that experience.

Though the wind can't be controlled, its power can be harnessed and used to bring energy for all life where it is needed. So, too, the energy of the Spirit is not just a personal experience but a source of divine power given to bring all life to greater fullness.

Reflection

May the power of the Spirit carry the fragile seeds of our faith to the place of growth.

MS

Not to condemn, but to love

'For God so loved the world that he gave his only Son, so that every-one who believes in him may not perish but may have eternal life. Indeed, God did not send the Son into the world to condemn the world, but in order that the world might be saved through him. Those who believe in him are not condemned; but those who do not believe are condemned already, because they have not believed in the name of the only Son of God. And this is the judgment, that the light has come into the world, and people loved darkness rather than light because their deeds were evil. For all who do evil hate the light and do not come to the light, so that their deeds may not be exposed. But those who do what is true come to the light, so that it may be clearly seen that their deeds have been done in God.'

It begins with love, John tells us— God's love for his creation. This is a mind-blowing truth because, for very many people, this is not their experience of human relationships. Very few of us ever experience the power of unconditional love. Even the love of parent for child is rarely, if ever, totally unconditional. Here we are told that God's love is poured out unstintingly and unconditionally, to the very limits of giving and forgiving.

Love desires to build up the other and bring him or her to full-ness of life, but so many human relationships are instead under-mined by criticism, judgment, rejection, condemnation. Here we are told that this isn't at all what Jesus is about. This truth can take a lifetime to assimilate, especially if we have lived with destructive crit-icism in our own relationships.

A child who is given this kind of loving affirmation learns to trust. God invites our trust. He invites us to go beyond merely believing facts about him in our head, to trusting him in our heart, with every breath we take. So it is that, in these few verses, John spells out the core of the gospel: God's love enables us to learn to trust first God, then each other and ourselves, and trust dispels fear.

Reflection

Where there is love, trust can grow. Where there is trust, fear of the darkness will fade into everlasting light.

MS

Jeremiah: man and message

Jeremiah's reputation is of a miserable prophet of doom and gloom. That he had a sombre message for the people of Jerusalem and Judah cannot be denied. Unless they repented of their disobedience, a terrible fate awaited them at the hands of the Babylonians. Events proved that Jeremiah was right: the people didn't repent and the Babylonians conquered their land.

A similar fate had already befallen Israel—the ten tribes occupying the northern part of the once united kingdom. They had been conquered by the Assyrians around 722BC. Josiah, however, the king of Judah (the remaining two tribes, centred on Jerusalem), had the wisdom to see that reformation was necessary if a similar fate was to be avoided and, for a while, he was able to root out from his people the idolatry, apathy and neglect of the Law that had cost their northern neighbours so dear. Eventually, Josiah was killed in battle fighting the Egyptians and the people quickly slipped back into their bad old ways.

During this period, Jeremiah had come on to the scene. The new king, Jehoiakim, was in effect an Egyptian puppet and, when Egypt was defeated by the Babylonians, he wisely submitted to the new rulers.

Rather less wisely, three years later, he decided to rebel against them. The Babylonians laid siege to Jerusalem. Jehoiakim died and was succeeded by Jehoiachin (sometimes called Jeconiah in NRSV). The city fell, the king was taken into exile and his uncle Zedekiah put on the throne of the conquered city. Against Jeremiah's advice, he led a rebellion against the Babylonians who returned to conquer the city in 586BC. It remained under Babylonian rule for nearly 50 years.

Jeremiah spoke the truth, fearlessly and without regard for his own safety. Consequently, like many before and after him, he was disowned by former friends in high places, subjected to public ridicule and even thrown into a muddy cistern. He spoke an 'inconvenient truth'. Yet, as we shall see, the book of Jeremiah is by no means all doom and gloom. Constantly the prophet holds before the people an alternative to the disaster threatening them—if they will only return to the Lord, then joy and prosperity will be their reward. It's no exaggeration to say that some of the Bible's most wonderful images of blessing are to be found in the oracles of this alleged prophet of despair.

David Winter

A prophet to the nations

Now the word of the Lord came to me saying, 'Before I formed you in the womb I knew you, and before you were born I consecrated you; I appointed you a prophet to the nations.' Then I said, 'Ah, Lord God! Truly I do not know how to speak, for I am only a boy.' But the Lord said to me, 'Do not say, "I am only a boy"; for you shall go to all to whom I send you, and you shall speak whatever I command you. Do not be afraid of them, for I am with you to deliver you, says the Lord.' Then the Lord put out his hand and touched my mouth; and the Lord said to me, 'Now I have put my words in your mouth.'

A prophet, in the biblical sense of the word, is not someone whose principal task is to foresee the future but 'forth tell' the word of the Lord. It was always seen as an awesome responsibility, which may account for Jeremiah's hesitancy here on the grounds of his youth. The Lord actually comforts him before his anxiety is expressed: 'Before you were born I… appointed you a prophet'. God's calling isn't dictated by age or experience, it's the vocation that counts.

Jeremiah's objection is simply swept aside. He has been called and for the most demanding of tasks—to be a prophet 'to the nations'. His message from God would not be just for the people of Judah or Israel but also for the Gentiles. His commission was from Yahweh, the eternal 'I AM', who revealed himself to Moses at the burning bush (see Exodus 3).

Whenever our Bibles spell 'the Lord' with capital letters, as they do here in verse 4, it is that sacred name that is being invoked.

The God of Abraham, Isaac and Jacob has a message for the whole earth, a message so powerful and so precious that the one who is to bear it was prepared for the task before he was born. Now, in Jeremiah's vision, the Lord God himself places that message in his mouth. From now on it's not 'This is the word of Jeremiah', but 'this is the word of the Lord'.

Reflection

God speaks through individuals, but his message is for the whole world.

DW

Watching over the word

The word of the Lord came to me, saying, 'Jeremiah, what do you see?' And I said, 'I see a branch of an almond tree.' Then the Lord said to me, 'You have seen well, for I am watching over my word to perform it.' The word of the Lord came to me a second time, saying, 'What do you see?' And I said, 'I see a boiling pot, tilted away from the north.' Then the Lord said to me: Out of the north disaster shall break out on all the inhabitants of the land.

The Hebrew prophets dealt in visions—they were 'seers', people who 'see'. Often, as here, the visions were of everyday things—an almond tree in blossom and a cooking pot tilted dangerously on the fire, so that when it boils its scalding contents will spill out. The prophets saw beyond the everyday, however. Everything they saw was pregnant with the purposes of God.

In these visions, two profound truths are spelt out. The first is based on a pun. The Hebrew word for 'almond tree' is very similar to the word for 'watching'. The vision of the almond tree reminds Jeremiah that God 'watches over' his word to ensure that it is fulfilled.

The boiling pot is more straightforward. It is tilted away from the north, so its contents will spill over the south. The application of this to the two kingdoms at that time is obvious. Israel, the northern ten tribes, has already been conquered. Now the threat shifts to the two tribes of Judah. Without swift repentance, the God who 'watches over' his word will allow the boiling pot to tip and they too will be invaded and conquered.

We shall see these two great themes being worked out all through the story of Jeremiah. The first is God's purpose, expressed in his 'word'. What God wills, happens. If it is conditional, it happens only if the conditions are fulfilled. The second is the law of consequence: if you do that, this will inevitably follow. Both are as true now as they were 2500 years ago.

Reflection

We live in a society that obstinately ignores the law of consequence. Actions bring reactions. Constantly God warns and we constantly fail to heed the warning. May God help us to see that what we do now influences what happens next!

DW

Good things defiled

The word of the Lord came to me, saying: Go and proclaim in the hearing of Jerusalem, Thus says the Lord: I remember the devotion of your youth, your love as a bride, how you followed me in the wilderness, in a land not sown... I brought you into a plentiful land to eat its fruits and its good things. But when you entered you defiled my land, and made my heritage an abomination. The priests did not say, 'Where is the Lord?' Those who handle the law did not know me; the rulers transgressed against me; the prophets prophesied by Baal, and went after things that do not profit.

Most of us would relate to the experience described here. We all know how easy it is to lose the youthful enthusiasm of faith, and to slip, almost without realising it, into a kind of routine religiosity. Jeremiah reminds his hearers in Jerusalem of the devotion of their ancestors, who followed God's call into the wilderness, eventually to enter the land 'flowing with milk and honey' (see Exodus 3:8 and elsewhere). They had no idea what lay ahead, but, trustingly, they followed. (Readers of the Exodus story will be aware that this is a rather rose-tinted picture of their behaviour!)

Now, five centuries or so later, the charge is that the descendants of the original settlers have defiled the promised land. Instead of making it into a place where the Lord was honoured, his Law obeyed and his covenant kept, they behaved as though it was their playground. They aped their pagan neighbours,

the prophets have prophesied by the heathen god Baal, the priests and law-makers have colluded in neglect and disobedience. Instead of eating 'its fruits and its good things', they are feasting on polluted food.

It's a sad indictment of the perils of that old term 'back-sliding'—falling away from where we were and know we ought to be. It's not an experience unique to ancient Israel and Judah, by any means. All of us who call ourselves disciples of Jesus need to check constantly that we are moving forward in faith and love, rather than gently, imperceptibly, slipping back into compromise and disobedience.

Reflection

Look into the mirror of God's perfect law of liberty (James 1:24–25) and check whether the progress is forwards or backwards.

DW

The cracked cisterns

Has a nation changed its gods, even though they are no gods? But my people have changed their glory for something that does not profit. Be appalled, O heavens, at this, be shocked, be utterly desolate, says the Lord, for my people have committed two evils: they have forsaken me, the fountain of living water, and dug out cisterns for themselves, cracked cisterns that can hold no water.

Jeremiah's charge against the people of Judah is far-reaching and serious. Why, he says, even the pagan nations don't change their gods (even though they're not 'proper' gods at all!), yet this people, called and cherished by the Lord, have abandoned him—their 'glory'—for something with no value. It still happens, of course—people who have known the Lord still turn away from him. An unhelpful relationship, a new hobby, a fear of being considered 'odd' or 'pious', even a preference for the conviviality of the pub or club over the fellowship of the church, it's fairly trivial things like these that can undermine a fragile faith. The prophet would say that such people have abandoned 'glory' for 'something that does not profit'.

Jeremiah applies a telling metaphor—particularly telling in a land where water is scarce and precious. Instead of drawing water from the inexhaustible spring ('living water'), the the people have hoarded this precious resource in cisterns that are leaky. A cracked cistern is a big inconvenience in a Western country today, but it was a total disaster in a hot, dry one like Judah. The 'fountain' of God's supply is plentiful, fresh and life-giving. The cisterns they have chosen are unreliable and will soon be empty.

The people would have understood this metaphor very clearly, but whether or not they were prepared to recognise that their cisterns were cracked or admit the superiority of a fresh spring is another matter. So often, for all of us, the immediate takes precedence over the ultimate. It may be a long walk to the spring, but at least when you get there there's water!

Reflection

As so often, our choices in life are crucial. Here, the choice is between the 'living water' of a covenant relationship with God and the stale liquid in leaking tanks. How amazing, says Jeremiah, that you have chosen the latter!

DW

Return and be healed

I thought how I would set you among my children, and give you a pleasant land, the most beautiful heritage of all the nations. And I thought you would call me, My Father, and would not turn from following me. Instead, as a faithless wife leaves her husband, so you have been faithless to me, O house of Israel, says the Lord. A voice on the bare heights is heard, the plaintive weeping of Israel's children, because they have perverted their way, they have forgotten the Lord their God: Return, O faithless children, I will heal your faithlessness. 'Here we come to you; for you are the Lord our God. Truly the hills are a delusion, the orgies on the mountains. Truly in the Lord our God is the salvation of Israel.'

This is like a scene from a play. From one direction, perhaps from the heights, comes the voice of God. He speaks of his hopes for this people, whom he had called to be his own—how they would be his children living in a pleasant land he had provided for them. But, the voice continues, it hasn't turned out like that. Like a wife who is unfaithful to her husband, they have turned away from him. The voice is plaintive rather than chiding, disappointed rather than angry.

Then we hear other sounds, perhaps from the far side—the bitter weeping of a people who recognise that they have made an appalling mistake. Their weeping is met by an invitation: 'Return and be healed.'

Then we see the people, perhaps now centre stage. With new insight they have seen their situation. The attraction of the heathen altars on the hillsides was illusory; the orgies they joined in were a delusion. Now they can see the truth: 'The Lord our God is the salvation of Israel!'

Sadly, this vision did not materialise. The people didn't repent; they remained blind to the folly and error of their ways, heedlessly plunging on towards disaster. It was not what God wanted and it was not what Jeremiah had hoped for, but it was their choice.

Reflection

Right to the bitter end, God held out to his people the hope of healing and restoration. It is never 'too late' to turn to God.

DW

In the gate of the temple

Thus says the Lord of hosts, the God of Israel: Amend your ways and your doings, and let me dwell with you in this place. Do not trust in these deceptive words: 'This is the temple of the Lord, the temple of the Lord, the temple of the Lord.' For if you truly amend your ways and your doings, if you truly act justly one with another, if you do not oppress the alien, the orphan, and the widow, or shed innocent blood in this place, and if you do not go after other gods to your own hurt, then I will dwell with you in this place, in the land that I gave of old to your ancestors for ever and ever.

The great temple in Jerusalem, first built by Solomon, was one of the wonders of the ancient world, but now, says the word of the Lord through Jeremiah, it has become a meaningless shrine. The people make their incantations, but they have forgotten the nature of the one whose presence among them it is intended to symbolise. God dwells with those who 'walk blamelessly' (Psalm 15:2), and they alone enjoy the blessing of his presence.

In other words, God's 'presence' among his people is conditional. He will be their God and Father, but only if they 'amend their ways and their doings'. In case that sounds a bit vague, some examples of what he requires of them are listed. They must 'act justly to one another', respect the alien, the orphan and the widow and not shed innocent blood. These are moral choices, but a profoundly 'religious' one is added: they must not 'go after other gods'—presumably those of the surrounding nations. It's reasonable to assume that these were some of the ways in which the people of Judah were already offending.

God may be wielding a stick, but there is also a juicy carrot to be had! If they correct these sins, God will 'dwell with them in this place', as he had done with their ancestors. The temple would once again truly be a house of God.

Reflection

The earthly temple was a reminder that God was in the midst of his people—not a distant deity but a living presence. A time would come when God would be located in neither Jerusalem nor Samaria, but in hearts that worshipped him 'in spirit and truth' (John 4:23).

DW

Good for nothing

Then I went to the Euphrates, and dug, and I took the loincloth from the place where I had hidden it. But now the loincloth was ruined; it was good for nothing. Then the word of the Lord came to me: Thus says the Lord: Just so I will ruin the pride of Judah and the great pride of Jerusalem. This evil people, who refuse to hear my words, who stubbornly follow their own will and have gone after other gods to serve them and worship them, shall be like this loincloth, which is good for nothing. For as the loincloth clings to one's loins, so I made the whole house of Israel and the whole house of Judah cling to me, says the Lord, in order that they might be for me a people, a name, a praise, and a glory.

The Hebrew prophets often used such visual prophecies. They were more than 'visual aids', because they didn't simply illustrate the message; they *were* the message. This is one of the most bizarre examples, however. Jeremiah took a loincloth and buried it 'by the river Euphrates'. As the river is about 400 miles from Jerusalem, in Babylon, we can probably assume that he didn't actually go there, but chose the place name because Babylon was a land of captivity for the Jews.

A loincloth was a basic undergarment. As Jeremiah explains, 'the loincloth clings to one's loins'—the nearest modern equivalent would be a pair of pants. He left it buried under the soil in a cleft of the rock and it stayed there for 'many days' (v. 6). Then he returned and dug it up. Not surprisingly, it was 'ruined', 'good for nothing'. The soil, the damp and probably a few insects had done their worst.

'The word of the Lord' came to Jeremiah. The fate of the rebellious people would be like that of the loincloth. As the loincloth was made to cling to the human body, so Israel and Judah were intended to cling to the Lord, to be a people who would bring him praise and glory. Detached from him, they were 'good for nothing'.

Reflection

As Jesus said, 'apart from me, you can do nothing' (John 15:5). Loincloths and vines bring the same lesson: God clings to those who cling to him.

DW

In the house of the potter

I went down to the potter's house, and there he was working at his wheel. The vessel he was making of clay was spoiled in the potter's hand, and he reworked it into another vessel, as seemed good to him. Then the word of the Lord came to me: Can I not do with you, O house of Israel, just as this potter has done? says the Lord. Just like the clay in the potter's hand, so are you in my hand, O house of Israel. At one moment I may declare concerning a nation or a kingdom, that I will pluck up and break down and destroy it, but if that nation, concerning which I have spoken, turns from its evil, I will change my mind about the disaster that I intended to bring on it.

Potters would have been a common sight at that time. People would stop to watch as these craftsmen turned their wheels and shaped the wet clay into the chosen design. The potters knew what they were making, but even the most skilful ones sometimes found that what they had produced was not to their liking—perhaps it had a flaw or some error had occurred in the process. It had become what modern shops call 'seconds'—OK to the casual eye, but not to that of the expert.

The Lord had told Jeremiah to observe the potter at work and, as he did so, watching him remake a spoilt item, the 'word of the Lord' came to him. That was how God would deal with his people. If they persisted in evil, then, as with a flawed vessel, he would simply destroy them and start again. If they repented, the loving and skilful hands of the divine potter would reshape them to their proper form.

It is a parable of repentance and redemption. 'You are the potter, I am the clay', we sometimes sing, perhaps without fully realising the awesome truth behind those words. God is not satisfied with seconds; he wants the best. In order to get it, like the potter, he will work and re-work until the true 'vessel' appears.

Reflection

What the prophet said of a nation is also true of individuals (and churches). The process of refinement continues as long as those involved are prepared to be worked and reworked in God's hands.

DW

JEREMIAH 24:1, 3–7 (NRSV, ABRIDGED)

Two baskets of figs

The Lord showed me two baskets of figs placed before the temple of the Lord... And the Lord said to me, 'What do you see, Jeremiah?' I said, 'Figs, the good figs very good, and the bad figs very bad, so bad that they cannot be eaten.' Then the word of the Lord came to me: Thus says the Lord, the God of Israel: Like these good figs, so I will regard as good the exiles from Judah, whom I have sent away from this place to the land of the Chaldeans. I will set my eyes upon them for good, and I will bring them back to this land... I will give them a heart to know that I am the Lord; and they shall be my people and I will be their God, for they shall return to me with their whole heart.

This passage relates to the time when some people in Judah and Jerusalem, together with King Jeconiah, had been taken into captivity in Babylon. Others, still resident in the city, led by a new king, Zedekiah, had sought an alliance with Egypt, against Jeremiah's advice. They hoped it would protect them from falling further into the hands of the Babylonians.

Those two groups of people are represented by the two baskets of figs. One is full of good, ripe figs. The other contains rotten ones, unfit for human consumption. The baskets stood 'before the temple'— in other words, before the Lord, as signs of his judgment. The good figs, the prophet explains, were those who had submitted to the Babylonians (called 'Chaldeans' here) and been carried off into captivity. Eventually, they would be wonderfully restored. The Lord

God would give them 'new hearts', hearts to know him.

As the verses that follow those of our passage (vv. 8–10) indicate, however, those who had attempted to avoid God's judgment by making political and military alliances would find that their stratagems were ineffective. They would also fall into the hands of the Babylonians, who would return to conquer the city.

What is the message for those reading Jeremiah today? Most simply, that we can't avoid repentance by devices and stratagems. Sin needs to be faced, named and repented. There really is no alternative.

Reflection

Only those who have faced the truth about themselves can expect to find forgiveness, healing and help.

DW

A crucial choice

At the beginning of the reign of King Jehoiakim... this word came from the Lord... Stand in the court of the Lord's house, and speak to all the cities of Judah that come to worship in the house of the Lord; speak to them all the words that I command you; do not hold back a word. It may be that they will listen, all of them, and will turn from their evil way, that I may change my mind about the disaster that I intend to bring on them because of their evil doings. You shall say to them: Thus says the Lord: If you will not listen to me, to walk in my law that I have set before you, and to heed the words of my servants the prophets whom I send to you urgently—though you have not heeded—then I will make this house like Shiloh, and I will make this city a curse for all the nations of the earth.

The book of Jeremiah doesn't run on like an historical narrative. Chapter 26 begins a long section of the book that offers a kind of symposium of the prophecies that Jeremiah had made during the previous years, all spelling out his central message: unless the people repented of their sins, 'walked in God's law' and 'heeded the words of his servants the prophets', disaster would befall them. This 'word' came at the beginning of the reign of Jehoiakim—during which the Babylonians captured Jerusalem and a sequence of events began that ended in the total subjugation of the people of Judah.

Jeremiah's message at this moment was crucial. The people were at a point of no return. They could repent and submit to God's purposes for them, which would be to their ultimate good, or they could go on as they had been and suffer the consequences. To follow or not to follow? To obey or not to obey? To trust or not to trust? These are the choices constantly put before us by God. The choice is ours, as it was for the people of Jerusalem over 2500 years ago.

Reflection

Choices have consequences. It's a lesson as old as the Garden of Eden, but just as relevant to us today. Deciding not to choose is not a way out but in itself a choice!

DW

Plans for your welfare

For surely I know the plans I have for you, says the Lord, plans for your welfare and not for harm, to give you a future with hope. Then when you call upon me and come and pray to me, I will hear you. When you search for me, you will find me; if you seek me with all your heart, I will let you find me, says the Lord, and I will restore your fortunes and gather you from all the nations and all the places where I have driven you, says the Lord, and I will bring you back to the place from which I sent you into exile.

According to the *Oxford Concise English Dictionary* a 'Jeremiah' is a person who 'complains continually or foretells disaster'. In the light of this beautiful prophecy of hope and blessing, it perhaps owes him an expanded entry, adding, 'Sometimes a person who sees a bright light in the darkness'.

In our passage, the prophet is addressing those who have been carried off into captivity in Babylon, whom he has already addressed as the heirs of a glorious future. Having submitted to God's judgment, they will come to enjoy his favour.

These blessings are not without conditions, however. The people must 'seek him'—and seek him 'with all your heart'. This describes the genuine longing for God that is always key to spiritual discovery. 'If you seek me,' says God, 'I will let you find me'—what an interesting phrase! The invisible, eternal God, the creator of the universe, the Father of Jesus, will 'let' us find him if we genuinely long to do so.

God had plans for these people. Plans for their welfare were being formulated in the heavens even while they were groaning in exile. It must have been hard for them to believe that despite all the terrible events that had overtaken them, which they could now see were self-inflicted, their God had not abandoned them. They were still his people, and he was still their God.

Reflection

When we speak of God's 'plans' for us, we don't mean that God has every detail of our lives organised, so that we are simply pawns on a chess board. His 'plans' require our cooperation, our heartfelt longing to find and know him and our willingness to walk the path he has chosen for us.

DW

A long-term investment

I bought the field at Anathoth from my cousin Hanamel, and weighed out the money to him, seventeen shekels of silver... and I gave the deed of purchase to Baruch... in the presence of my cousin Hanamel, in the presence of the witnesses who signed the deed of purchase, and in the presence of all the Judeans who were sitting in the court of the guard. In their presence I charged Baruch, saying, Thus says the Lord of hosts, the God of Israel: Take these deeds, both this sealed deed of purchase and this open deed, and put them in an earthenware jar, in order that they may last for a long time.

This strange incident makes little sense detached from the history of the time. Jerusalem was under siege and Jeremiah had warned that it would soon fall into the hands of the Babylonians. For many years the land would be worthless, the fields untilled, the houses deserted. This was not a sensible time to be buying land or property, yet here is Jeremiah, prompted by God, publicly buying a field, paying cash for it and having the sale legally recorded. Most people would describe that as a disastrous investment!

It is, of course, another of the dramatic 'acted prophecies' that mark this book. His purchase of the field was a practical witness to his faith that God had not finally abandoned his people. Indeed, further on in this chapter the word of the Lord promises that, at some future time, 'Just as I have brought all this great disaster upon this people, so I will bring upon them all the good fortune that I now promise them. Fields shall be bought in this land of which you are saying, It is a desolation' (vv. 42–43). Jeremiah's 'investment' proved a long-term one—it was actually over 50 years before the field was a valuable asset again—but it was as secure as the promises of the God he served. By then, Jeremiah himself had died, but the deeds so carefully drawn up, witnessed and stored stood as evidence of the faithfulness of God.

Reflection

We live in an instant age, when people tend to pursue short-term goals, but the life of faith is essentially a long-term 'investment', involving storing up 'treasures in heaven', as Jesus called it (Matthew 6:20).

DW

A call to surrender

Then Jeremiah said to Zedekiah, 'Thus says the Lord… If you will only surrender to the officials of the king of Babylon, then your life shall be spared, and this city shall not be burned with fire, and you and your house shall live. But if you do not surrender to the officials of the king of Babylon, then this city shall be handed over to the Chaldeans, and they shall burn it with fire, and you yourself shall not escape from their hand.' King Zedekiah said to Jeremiah, 'I am afraid of the Judeans who have deserted to the Chaldeans, for I might be handed over to them and they would abuse me.' Jeremiah said, 'That will not happen. Just obey the voice of the Lord in what I say to you, and it shall go well with you, and your life shall be spared.'

We are now in the final stages of Jeremiah's story. Jerusalem is under siege by the Babylonians. The king of Judah, Zedekiah, is terrified, both of falling into the enemy's hands and of abuse at the hands of those of his people who have already gone over to the enemy's side. He has unsuccessfully tried various stratagems and alliances and certainly was not keen on following Jeremiah's advice, though it had at least been consistent all along. The Babylonians were the instruments of God's righteous judgment of his rebellious people and the wisest course of action was to surrender to them and trust that God would eventually deliver his people.

We can sense Zedekiah's fear. It would be a brave decision to surrender to the enemy—conquered kings generally got short shrift in the ancient world. On the other hand, his options were few. Jeremiah promised him that if he did this, his life—and the city itself—would be spared the otherwise inevitable torching and looting. 'Just obey the word of the Lord', the prophet urged, 'and it shall go well with you'.

The promise was clear enough, but Zedekiah ignored it. Against Jeremiah's advice, he attempted a rebellion against the Babylonians, which was easily defeated. He and his band were pursued out of the city and caught. The victors took him captive and blinded him.

Reflection

Sometimes the least attractive path turns out to be the one that leads to life.

DW

The 'if' test

Then all the commanders of the forces... and all the people from the least to the greatest, approached the prophet Jeremiah and said, 'Be good enough to listen to our plea, and pray to the Lord your God for us—for all this remnant. For there are only a few of us left out of many, as your eyes can see. Let the Lord your God show us where we should go and what we should do.' ... At the end of ten days the word of the Lord came to Jeremiah. Then he... said to [the people], 'Thus says the Lord, the God of Israel, to whom you sent me to present your plea before him: If you will only remain in this land, then I will build you up and not pull you down; I will plant you, and not pluck you up; for I am sorry for the disaster that I have brought upon you.'

At the end of our readings from Jeremiah, we are still in the same position as we were at the start. It all turns on the little but crucial word 'if'. There is a party of Jews who are minded to flee to Egypt to escape from the Babylonians and rebuild their lives there. Before deciding to go, they ask Jeremiah for divine guidance. Their request is perfectly couched—'show us where we should go and what we should do'. The prophet treated their request seriously, but it took him ten days to come back with the Lord's answer: we sometimes have to wait for divine guidance!

The guidance that came was probably not what they wanted to hear. If they will remain in Judah, under Babylonian occupation, God will build them up and not pull them down. He is 'sorry' for the awful, though inevitable, events that have come to the land. If they stay, God will save and rescue them (v. 11), but it all hinges on their decision. The 'if' is a very big one!

Reflection

Against Jeremiah's advice, they decided to go to Egypt, thus contradicting a command given to Israel when God brought them out of Egypt: they were to 'never return that way again' (Deuteronomy 17:16). They failed the 'if' test— neither the first nor the last of God's people to do so.

DW

True or false? The letter of Jude

Queuing in a shop one day, I saw the man ahead of me pass a £20 note to the assistant in payment for his purchase. She held it in her hand for a brief moment, then handed it back. 'That's not real,' she said matter-of-factly. Embarrassed, the man opened his wallet and gave her another note, which this time she accepted.

Afterwards I asked the assistant how she knew that it was not a genuine note. 'When you handle money all day,' she said, 'you can tell simply by the feel whether it is real or not.'

Within a short time of the Church coming into being, false teachings were corrupting the pure message of the gospel—an obvious strategy by Satan to frustrate the work of God.

Jude wrote his letter to help his readers develop the gift of spiritual discernment, to be able to recognise false teachers when they appeared and distinguish the real from the counterfeit.

The gift of discernment is just as needed in our day. We are to be open to whatever God is doing, but we must be neither naïve or gullible. False teachers are still at work and we must know how to evaluate what we hear. A plethora of ideas reaches us nowadays through the Internet, satellite TV, books and DVDs, magazines and other publications, conferences and seminars. It is vital that we discern what is of God and what is not.

Jude (a shortened form of Judas) appears to have been the brother of James, the leader of the early Church (Acts 15:13; Galatians 1:19), and therefore a half-brother of Jesus (Matthew 13:55; Mark 6:3). He seems to have been an itinerant teacher, writing in the last quarter of the first century for an audience of believers with a strong Jewish background. He found himself rather reluctantly having to defend the truth of the gospel and identify and expose certain false teachers who were leading them astray.

This tiny epistle has a chequered history, only being accepted into the canon of scripture at a relatively late date, but there is no reason to doubt its authenticity or inspiration. While it is not an easy read, packed as it is with obscure references to Jewish history and tradition, it nevertheless contains some spiritual gems and will help us become more discerning ourselves.

Tony Horsfall

Good foundations

Jude, a servant of Jesus Christ and a brother of James, To those who have been called, who are loved by God the Father and kept by Jesus Christ: Mercy, peace and love be yours in abundance.

Every building needs a good foundation and, to withstand the storms, it must rest on solid ground. Likewise, when the winds of false doctrine are swirling all around, it is important that believers are firmly grounded in Christ.

Jude does not claim any special privileges because of his earthly relationship to Jesus. He relates to him now like anyone else, in a spiritual way and as a servant. He himself is resting on the solid ground that is Christ. His readers, too, have a firm foundation. Three verbs emphasise the divine activity in their lives and remind them of their security.

Looking back, they have been *called* to follow Jesus, just as the first disciples were—a calling that originated in the will of God, not in their own desire. His divine faithfulness assures them that, having called them, he will accompany them all the way.

Presently, and for now and eternity, they are *loved*. They have the unchanging and everlasting love of the Father, which means that they are forever within his grip of grace. Nothing will be able to separate them from his great love.

In the future, they will be *kept* —watched over and cared for by the shepherd and guardian of their souls, Jesus Christ himself. No matter what testings, trials or temptations come their way, he is there to protect them.

Knowing the pressures that the believers are facing, Jude offers a simple prayer for them, asking that a trio of wonderful gifts be theirs— mercy for their mistakes, peace for their circumstances and love for their relationships. Also, rather than asking for an incremental increase in such blessings, he calls for these gifts to be theirs in abundance—or, more literally, that they will be 'multiplied' to them in extravagant generosity.

Isn't it encouraging to know that we, too, can build on such solid ground and these same blessings are available for us today?

Prayer

Lord, help me to build my faith on the solid ground that is in Christ, and not rely on the shifting sands of this world.

TH

Danger—beware!

Dear friends, although I was very eager to write to you about the salvation we share, I felt I had to write and urge you to contend for the faith that was once for all entrusted to the saints. For certain persons whose condemnation was written about long ago have secretly slipped in among you. They are godless people, who change the grace of our God into a licence for immorality and deny Jesus Christ our only Sovereign and Lord.

Jude acknowledges that he has had a change of plans. He had intended to write a devotional letter full of encouragement. Now, because of what he has heard of the subversive activities of the false teachers, he finds himself writing in a confrontational style in order to make a robust defence of the faith that is under fire.

Jude never identifies the false teachers explicitly—he does not 'name and shame' them—but, presumably, they would be easily identified by his hearers. What they are teaching, moreover, is abundantly clear.

First, they have changed the liberating teaching of grace into an excuse for licentiousness. Grace frees us from keeping the law in order to be saved or earn God's favour, but it does not liberate us from living a holy life. These teachers were turning liberty into licence and thereby excusing their immoral ways. Jude responds as the apostle Paul would: 'Are we to continue in sin that grace may abound? By no means!' (Romans 6:1, RSV).

Second, they deny the lordship of Jesus Christ. This might mean denying that Jesus is the Son of God (a common first-century heresy), but it is more likely to mean that they did not allow him to be Lord of their lives. They wanted to decide for themselves how they should behave, declaring a moral autonomy that allowed them to live as they pleased, with disastrous results.

Such teaching can never square with the true gospel as taught by the apostles and Jude found himself having to take a stand against it. He was not looking for a fight, but he knew that so much was at stake here he was compelled to stand up for that which he knew to be true.

Prayer

Lord, show me when to stand up and be counted.

TH

A serious matter

Though you already know all this, I want to remind you that the Lord delivered his people out of Egypt, but later destroyed those who did not believe. And the angels who did not keep their positions of authority but abandoned their own home—these he has kept in darkness, bound with everlasting chains for judgment on the great day. In a similar way, Sodom and Gomorrah and the surrounding towns gave themselves up to sexual immorality and perversion. They serve as an example of those who suffer the punishment of eternal fire.

It is bad enough to go astray oneself, but to mislead others and do so deliberately, with a clear intention, is an altogether more serious matter. This explains the anger that Jude directs towards the godless men who have abused their place of trust. Those who teach have a great responsibility and will be judged with greater strictness (James 3:1).

Jude's knowledge of the Old Testament shines through here and suggests that his readers would have been familiar with the great stories from Israel's past, of which three examples are given.

Despite having been miraculously rescued from Egypt, the people of Israel refused to believe that God could bring them to the promised land. Led by the unbelieving spies, they rebelled against the leadership of Moses, threatening to stone him. As a result, that whole generation died in the wilderness (see Numbers 13 and 14).

The angelic rebellion that Jude speaks about is somewhat hard to pin down, but it may refer to the uprising that accompanied Lucifer's ambitious attempt to overthrow God's authority, possibly hinted at in Isaiah 14:12–15 and Ezekiel 28:11–19. They refused to keep the places assigned to them by God and, as a result, are now awaiting judgment (see also 2 Peter 2:4).

The people of Sodom and Gomorrah, likewise, rebelled, overthrowing God's moral standards and choosing instead the most debased and perverted lifestyle. The outcome was that their cities were destroyed by fire (see Genesis 19).

The implication is clear: God will not be mocked. Those who deliberately pervert the truth and lead others astray will answer to him.

Reflection

'The fear of the Lord is the beginning of knowledge' (Proverbs 1:7).

TH

Acting according to type

In the very same way, these dreamers pollute their own bodies, reject authority and slander celestial beings. But even the archangel Michael, when he was disputing with the devil about the body of Moses, did not dare to bring a slanderous accusation against him, but said, 'The Lord rebuke you!' Yet these people speak abusively against whatever they do not understand; and what things they do understand by instinct, like unreasoning animals—these are the very things that destroy them. Woe to them! They have taken the way of Cain; they have rushed for profit into Balaam's error; they have been destroyed in Korah's rebellion.

How can we recognise false teachers? By the way they behave. They always act according to type. Like the people of Sodom, they sin against their bodies by means of sexual misconduct. Like the fallen angels, they refuse to submit to authority. Like the Israelites in the desert, they slander other people.

The reference to the archangel Michael and the dispute over the body of Moses is taken from an apocryphal book, *The Assumption of Moses*. The point is that even an angel as authoritative as Michael was careful not to overstep his position. The false teachers show no such restraint. Instead, their abusive words flow freely, condemning themselves. Their real motivations are exposed by their actions and they fall into the traps that caught out other godless men before them.

Like murderous Cain, they operate on a purely instinctual level, out of envy, greed and anger. They are not led by the Spirit, but are dominated by the flesh (see Genesis 4:1–16; 1 John 3:12).

Like greedy Balaam, they are motivated by material gain. Balaam allowed himself to be hired to speak against Israel for financial reward and these men follow a similar path (see Numbers 22—24; 2 Peter 2:15–16).

Like self-promoting Korah, they are driven by personal ambition. Korah led a revolt against the leadership of Moses and he and his followers perished as a result (see Numbers 16). Likewise, the false teachers have overthrown apostolic authority in their desire for power and position.

Prayer
Lord, help me to be godly, not godless.

TH

By their fruits

These people are blemishes at your love feasts, eating with you without the slightest qualm—shepherds who feed only themselves. They are clouds without rain, blown along by the wind; autumn trees, without fruit and uprooted—twice dead. They are wild waves of the sea, foaming up their shame; wandering stars, for whom blackest darkness has been reserved for ever... These people are grumblers and fault-finders; they follow their own evil desires; they boast about themselves and flatter others for their own advantage.

According to Jesus, the best way to identify false prophets is to examine the fruit of their lives and ministry (Matthew 7:15–20). This may not be immediately evident, but, over a period of time, it will be seen whether they are producing good fruit or bad. When this acid test is applied to the teachers Jude has in his mind, they fail miserably.

They are not good shepherds because they think only of themselves and do nothing to nurture those under their care. They promise much, but deliver little of true spiritual refreshment to their thirsty hearers. They are unproductive when it comes to bearing the fruit of the Spirit in their lives. There is simply no spiritual life in them.

Their true nature is revealed over time. Just as the ocean tide eventually throws up its flotsam and jetsam, so the corruption within these men surfaces after a while. They appear good on the outside, but soon their wickedness is exposed.

Like shooting stars, they begin well but soon burn themselves out and their light is extinguished.

In contrast to these godless men, Jude reminds his hearers of a godly man—Enoch, the one who 'walked with God; then he was no more, because God took him' (Genesis 5:24, NRSV). Not only does Enoch condemn them by his example but also by his words. He predicted (in the apocryphal book *1 Enoch*) a day of judgment when the ungodly will answer to God for their words and actions (Jude 14–15).

Jude then gives us two ways to achieve discernment. First, ask 'How do these people behave? What motivates them?' Second, ask 'What fruit is being produced in their lives? What is their legacy?' These are searching questions, for all of us.

Prayer

Cause me to bear good fruit for you, Lord.

TH

JUDE 17–23 (NIV)

The best antidote

But, dear friends, remember what the apostles of our Lord Jesus Christ foretold. They said to you, 'In the last times there will be scoffers who will follow their own ungodly desires.' These are the people who divide you, who follow mere natural instincts and do not have the Spirit. But you, dear friends, build yourselves up in your most holy faith and pray in the Holy Spirit. Keep yourselves in God's love as you wait for the mercy of our Lord Jesus Christ to bring you to eternal life. Be merciful to those who doubt; snatch others from the fire and save them; to others show mercy, mixed with fear— hating even the clothing stained by corrupted flesh.

Jude can now return, briefly, to his original desire to share with his hearers positive truths about their salvation. They should not be surprised to find themselves embattled with false teachers, but the best way to overcome them is to concentrate on growing in their own faith. He suggests four practical things that they can do.

They are encouraged to *build*. They already have a good foundation in Christ, but now they are to grow by nourishing themselves on the truths that make up the faith that they have received. Such truths need to be received inwardly (from the head to the heart) and applied outwardly (from theory to practice).

They are encouraged to *pray*. The Holy Spirit is our helper in every aspect of Christian living, but especially in the difficult area of prayer. He teaches us how to pray and energises us for the task, opening up for us the lines of communication with the living God.

They are encouraged *stay*. God has placed them in Christ and within the realm of his unchanging love. Now they are to abide there, make him their dwelling place and not wander off into a life of separation and independence.

They are to *wait*. Jesus is coming again and the awareness of his return should strengthen their resolve and fortify their hope. He will come back and they will share in his victory.

Nor are they to look out for themselves alone. Pastoral care in the church is a mutual thing and, in times of battle, we are to protect one another.

Prayer
Lord, keep me safe in you.

TH

Security

To him who is able to keep you from falling and to present you before his glorious presence without fault and with great joy—to the only God our Saviour be glory, majesty, power and authority, through Jesus Christ our Lord, before all ages, now and for evermore! Amen.

In such uncertain times, it would be easy for Jude's hearers to become anxious or afraid. How can they withstand the false teachers? How will they cope under such great pressure? Jude's confidence (and theirs) is in the saving power of God. Having taken hold of them, he will never let go.

Here on earth, he is able to keep them from falling or, more literally, 'tripping up'. Temptation is real and persistent and sin will always be waiting to catch them out (Genesis 4:7), but even when they are weak and vulnerable they need not fall, because the Lord is their keeper. Nor do they need to be afraid of falling prey to the deceitful wiles of the false teachers. God himself will expose the teachers' schemes and give the people the discernment they need to stand firm in their faith. The false teachers may try to trip up these young believers, but they will not cause them to stumble, because God is their protector.

One day the keeping power of God will be fully recognised. These embattled saints will make it triumphantly to the end, for they will not fall away. The one who began a good work in them will bring it to completion (Philippians 1:6). Having set out on the heavenly journey, they will arrive home safely because of his amazing grace. Through the blood of Jesus shed on the cross, they have been cleansed from every sin and will take their place in the presence of God with the joy of angelic songs resounding in their ears. This is their confidence and their hope.

These certainties are ours, too, because of our faith in Jesus Christ. They are true for all ages and in all places. We can sing this magnificent doxology and know that God is watching over us. We can live for his glory and worship his majesty. We can experience his power and submit to his authority. It is our choice and the response of faith.

Prayer

*Lord, you are worthy of
all our praise!*

TH

'The quick and the dead'

The time around Hallowe'en (All Hallows Eve—the day before All Saints, or All Hallows, Day, 1 November) tends to be an uncomfortable one for Christians, in the UK anyway. While in the USA the custom of children dressing up as ghosts and witches in order to go out 'trick or treating' around the neighbourhood has mostly been seen as harmless fun, many UK churches tend to take a different view. Outreach events such as a 'Light Party' are increasingly popular, celebrating the coming of a Saviour, rather than revelling in the Dark Side.

Whatever your personal view on the matter, it is undeniable that these few days have now become another colossal sales opportunity. While health and safety issues have started to quench traditional Bonfire night festivities, plastic pumpkins, witches' hats and luminous skeletons start appearing on shop shelves before September is out.

Is it possible to reclaim this time as a chance to pause and reflect on mortality, on what will one day happen to every one of us and remember those known to us who have already died? It is often said that, these days, death is the Great Unmentionable, as sex used to be. In great contrast to the last century, many of us will reach mid-life before we experience the death of a close relative or friend. We are not familiar with death and dying and may very much prefer not to think about it at all until circumstances compel us to do so.

Over the next few days, though, we will reflect on a number of Bible passages relating in some way to dying, bereavement and the promise of eternal life. Some readers may find the topic uncomfortable—perhaps because they are anticipating or experiencing a painful bereavement. Some may shy away from the whole topic because, deep down, they feel it is just too frightening to contemplate. It is my hope and prayer that all who follow these readings may glean some encouragement, comfort or hope, whether for themselves or those whom they love and may be seeking to console during a difficult time.

A note about the title. The phrase 'the quick and the dead' keeps in use an otherwise obsolete meaning of 'quick'—the sense of 'alive' rather than 'speedy'. The phrase occurs in both the King James Version of the Bible and traditional versions of the Nicene and Apostles' Creeds.

Naomi Starkey

Running with perseverance

Therefore, since we are surrounded by such a great cloud of witnesses, let us throw off everything that hinders and the sin that so easily entangles. And let us run with perseverance the race marked out for us, fixing our eyes on Jesus, the pioneer and perfecter of faith. For the joy that was set before him he endured the cross, scorning its shame, and sat down at the right hand of the throne of God. Consider him who endured such opposition from sinners, so that you will not grow weary and lose heart.

Today is All Saints' Day, when many churches traditionally remember the 'blessed saints' (in the words of the Anglican prayer for today) and martyrs, while tomorrow we remember 'all the faithful departed'. The popular meaning of 'saint' is 'very holy, special person', but we should remember that Paul, for example, used the word simply to mean 'Christians' (see 1 Corinthians 16:15; 2 Corinthians 13:12).

Our passage follows one of the more extraordinary chapters in the New Testament—Hebrews 11's list of the heroes of faith from Abel onwards. We read (quite possibly open-mouthed) of those 'who were tortured… faced jeers and flogging… were put to death by stoning… sawn in two… killed by the sword' and so on (vv. 35–37). How can we ever measure up to the courage shown by such saints?

The answer comes in the first verse above: these people are part of a 'cloud' of witnesses, spectators in a heavenly stadium, cheering us on as we 'run… the race marked out for us'. Like good athletes, we need to keep our eyes on the finishing tape and who is there, ahead of us, urging us to keep going. Jesus himself is waiting, ready to welcome us as we complete the race in which he has already been victorious.

It is too easy for us to think of saints as superhuman, quite different from us, but we should remember that every one of them was an ordinary man or woman. What made the difference was their willingness to let God's power work through them, whatever the cost.

Reflection

Think about those heroes of faith—whether personally known to you or from the Bible or later history—whose example you find particularly inspiring. Then imagine them cheering you on to the end.

NS

A better place

For to me, to live is Christ and to die is gain. If I am to go on living in the body, this will mean fruitful labour for me. Yet what shall I choose? I do not know! I am torn between the two: I desire to depart and be with Christ, which is better by far.

All Souls' Day falls today. A lesser festival in the Church calendar and less well known than All Saints (and even less well known than the night before), it is a day set aside for remembering the dead. We are asked to think of not just our own loved ones but all those awaiting the day of resurrection.

The final words of our passage were familiar to me from a very early age because they are engraved on my grandparents' gravestone. For years I found the sentiment baffling, but I came to see why the idea of being 'in a better place' could provide some comfort, especially if the one who died had suffered much. It did little, though, to cheer up those whose overriding thoughts were along the lines of 'But I want them to stay and play with me!'

We need to linger over Paul's words here and ask why he should be 'torn between' death and life, how dying could possibly be 'gain', especially if it meant cutting short his missionary work before it was finished. The key comes in the final sentence: he looks forward to being 'with Christ'. Note the 'with': Paul is not hoping for a chance of hanging around an outer suburb of the heavenly city, on the off-chance of an occasional glimpse of the Prince of Peace. He is confident that after death he will find himself in his Lord's very presence.

That, of course, is 'better by far'. The original Greek words form a triple emphasis, a very strong affirmation—'unimaginably better', 'surpassing all expectations'. It may not console us much when our grief is raw, but it is a reminder that the grave is not the gateway to dust but to glory. If we believe in an eternal God, his love is not limited by space, time and mortality.

Reflection

The Bible does not tell us to pray for the dead, as many instinctively want to do, but we can thank God for their lives and entrust them into his gentle hands.

NS

God is there

Where can I go from your Spirit? Where can I flee from your presence? If I go up to the heavens, you are there; if I make my bed in the depths, you are there. If I rise on the wings of the dawn, if I settle on the far side of the sea, even there your hand will guide me, your right hand will hold me fast. If I say, 'Surely the darkness will hide me and the light become night around me,' even the darkness will not be dark to you; the night will shine like the day, for darkness is as light to you.

Our first two readings have focused on those who have died, but what about the living? What about those reading these notes today who may be struggling with a new bereavement or remembering a past loss? What about those who live in secret fear of ever having to face their own death or that of somebody they love?

These verses, from one of the best-known and loved of psalms, tell us that, wherever we go, whatever happens to us, the Lord God is with us. His presence suffuses the universe and it is not a brooding, shadowy presence, but a Father's infinitely caring touch.

The speaker may feel that everything is in disarray—'the darkness will hide me… the light become night around me'—but that is no obstacle to God. We should remember, too, that, in ancient Israel, the sea tended to be a troubling, rather than comforting, symbol. 'The far side of the sea'

implied not an exciting travel destination, but being cut off from God's people, banished beyond a watery expanse that was a reminder of pre-creation chaos. Even that remote place is not beyond God's reach, however.

The fog of deep grief—or fear—can make us feel as if we are trapped in a bad dream, unable to wake. The message here is that God's light cuts through the thickest fog, the densest darkness.

Reflection

'For I am convinced that neither death nor life, neither angels nor demons, neither the present nor the future, nor any powers, neither height nor depth, nor anything else in all creation, will be able to separate us from the love of God that is in Christ Jesus our Lord' (Romans 8:38–39).

NS

Gone but not forgotten

As a father has compassion on his children, so the Lord has compassion on those who fear him; for he knows how we are formed, he remembers that we are dust. As for mortals, their days are like grass, they flourish like a flower of the field; the wind blows over it and it is gone, and its place remembers it no more. But from everlasting to everlasting the Lord's love is with those who fear him, and his righteousness with their children's children.

A vicar I know once told me that the hardest funerals he ever had to conduct were those closest to his own family circumstances: a premature baby, a three-year-old boy and a teenager, all of whom died unexpectedly. With the funeral of an adult, especially an older adult, there could at least be a sense of long years well-lived. Seeing the sharp pain of a sudden loss, an abrupt ending long before maturity, was a reminder of why death often used to be caricatured as the Grim Reaper—a skeletal figure with a scythe that ruthlessly mowed down lives like so much grass.

This coming Sunday is Remembrance Sunday, a time to commemorate those cut down in war. I shall never forget a service of remembrance I once attended in a small village. Such a small village, but so many names to read from the war memorial and so many with the same surnames attending that simple service decades later.

Our passage today reminds us that God is like a compassionate father, turning to us with kindness because he knows how small and frail human beings are, so easily cut down like grass, blown away like straw on the wind. Right now you may be grieving for someone whose life seemed hopelessly brief or so anonymous that you feel you are the only one left to keep his or her memory alive, but take comfort from some words of Jesus. He told his disciples: 'Are not five sparrows sold for two pennies? Yet not one of them is forgotten by God... you are worth more than many sparrows' (Luke 12:6—7).

Reflection

It is probably unhelpful to think of those we mourn as people we have 'lost'. They are not with us any longer, but they are not lost—God has them and is keeping them safe.

NS

The resurrection and the life

Jesus said to [Martha], 'Your brother will rise again.' Martha answered, 'I know he will rise again in the resurrection at the last day.' Jesus said to her, 'I am the resurrection and the life. Anyone who believes in me will live, even though they die; and whoever lives by believing in me will never die. Do you believe this?' 'Yes, Lord,' she told him, 'I believe that you are the Messiah, the Son of God, who was to come into the world.'

This passage contains the fifth of Jesus' seven 'I am' sayings in John's Gospel (see also chapters. 6, 8, 10, 14 and 15). These words are well-known, too, as a traditional opening to a funeral service, as the minister receives the coffin into the church.

The impact of Jesus' statement can be diminished by overfamiliarity—we may fail to appreciate the intense drama of what took place that day in Bethany. This was Jesus' favourite bolt-hole, home of his best friends (v. 5), one of whom had died. Jesus had come too late to help, despite an urgent summons from the family (vv. 3, 17). When Martha, the dead man's sister, confronts Jesus with what has happened (v. 21), their exchange leads to Jesus' extraordinary claim and her declaration of faith in him as God's anointed one.

If we are tempted to think of this as a formal, calm exchange of words, we should read on a few verses to see how upset Jesus was by the situation. Richard Burridge, in his *People's Bible Commentary: John* (BRF, 1998), explains how the Greek phrase translated 'deeply moved in spirit and troubled' (v. 33) implied that Jesus was actually 'shuddering, shaking with emotions'. Burridge goes on: 'In Jesus, God has experienced the depths of the human condition, including pain, grief and love.'

Jesus' statement—'I am the resurrection and the life'—is not a clinical formula, but an urgent cry of hope in the face of despair. The Son of God, Lord of time and eternity, shook with emotion as he confronted death, seeing how it ripped the heart from a family. Then he acted decisively to reveal how the power of God within him was greater even than death, foreshadowing his own resurrection and the promise of eternal life to all who believe in him.

Reflection
'Do you believe this?' (John 11:26).

NS

1 Corinthians 15:50–52, 54–55 (TNIV)

At the last trumpet

I declare to you, brothers and sisters, that flesh and blood cannot inherit the kingdom of God, nor does the perishable inhabit the imperishable. Listen, I tell you a mystery: we will not all sleep, but we will all be changed—in a flash, in the twinkling of an eye, at the last trumpet. For the trumpet will sound, the dead will be raised imperishable, and we will be changed... When the perishable has been clothed with the imperishable, and the mortal with immortality, then the saying that is written will come true: 'Death has been swallowed up in victory.' 'Where, O death, is your victory? Where, O death, is your sting?'

The sounding of a trumpet to mark significant events was a regular part of life in ancient Israel (and still features in Jewish worship), but we should not think of a polished brass or silver orchestral instrument, but the *shofar*, or ram's horn. In Joel 2:1, for example, we read 'Blow the trumpet [*shofar*] in Zion' to mark 'the day of the Lord'. In Paul's lyrical description of the 'day of the Lord', the *shofar* rings out to herald the final revelation of the kingdom of God.

The implications of Jesus' resurrection are made clear: 'we will all be changed'. Jesus rose with a new body, identifiably himself, able to eat and drink, walk and talk with his friends. He was no longer limited by the laws of physics, but very definitely not a ghost either. Paul admits that this transformation is a 'mystery' but still something that he is confident to announce with boldness, drawing in quotes from

Isaiah (25:8) and Hosea (13:14) to support his case.

The promise of the resurrection of the dead is why people have traditionally been buried facing east (in line with the orientation of most churches), so that the gravestone is, in fact, placed at their feet rather than their head. The symbolism of this is profound: they sleep in the earth yet they face the rising sun, waiting for the day of the Lord and their rising to new life.

Reflection

In a flash, at a trumpet crash,
I am all at once what Christ is,
since he was what I am, and
This Jack, joke, poor potsherd, patch,
matchwood, immortal diamond,
Is immortal diamond.

Gerard Manley Hopkins, 'That Nature is a Heraclitean Fire' (1888)
NS

No more crying

'See, I will create new heavens and a new earth. The former things will not be remembered, nor will they come to mind. But be glad and rejoice for ever in what I will create, for I will create Jerusalem to be a delight and its people a joy... the sound of weeping and of crying will be heard in it no more... Before they call I will answer; while they are still speaking I will hear. The wolf and the lamb will feed together, and the lion will eat straw like an ox... They will neither harm nor destroy on all my holy mountain,' says the Lord.

This vision of the Lord God renewing creation and healing every hurt runs through the Bible like a golden thread. Those who first heard these words would have understood them as relating to the restoration of Israel following the catastrophe of the exile to Babylon, although such restoration would involve far more than a return to the splendour of even Solomon's reign (see 2 Chronicles 9). God says that 'the former things will not be remembered', such will be the glory of what is to come.

As we read this vision in the light of Jesus' death and resurrection, we look forward to the end of time and history when the Messiah returns to reign in a new Jerusalem to which 'the kings of the earth will bring their splendour' (Revelation 21:24). Instead of disembodied souls floating away to an ethereal realm (an ancient Greek idea), the Christian hope is of eternal life in a tangible, sensuous creation—but one transfigured by God's shining presence.

C.S. Lewis' novel *The Great Divorce* (1946) is a compelling picture of what this new creation could be like. It would be so vastly real and substantial that, by comparison, our present world would be like a faint shadow. This is not an argument for belittling what we now have as ultimately worthless, but a reminder that we should live in the awareness that one day our Father's promise to us of life everlasting will be fulfilled beyond our wildest imaginings.

Reflection

In sorrow we must go, but not in despair. Behold! We are not bound for ever to the circles of the world, and beyond them is more than memory.

J.R.R. Tolkien, *The Return of the King* (1955)

NS

Proverbs 17:1—22:16

The book of Proverbs is one of the two main works of the Wisdom tradition found in the Bible—the other is Ecclesiastes. Knowing something about this tradition is a great help in reading the book, which can otherwise seem like a rather random collection of sayings, some bafflingly obscure, others boringly obvious and others with great depth.

The Wisdom tradition takes a particular view of the world. It is one in which a sense of order is central and every action has a consequence, for good or for ill: 'The sayings of the wise have been transmitted by the elders, who are to be held in respect, and this world-sustaining wisdom of the sages is maintained through individual and social discipline. Wisdom thus affirms a divine cosmic order and represents folly as disorder' (Robert Alter and Frank Kermode, *The Literary Guide to the Bible*, Collins, 1987, p. 265).

Although there are some parts of Proverbs that can be read continuously (such as much of chapters 1—9 and 31:10–31, on the good wife), most of the book is a collection of individual sayings. Some commentators have tried to find shape and purpose in the way that they have been put together,

but most agree that this does not work. They are, in effect, soundbites, one-liners, and should be read as such.

Our chapters form part of the longest single section and the oldest part of the book, which runs from 10:1 to 22:16. It probably dates from before the Babylonian exile and, like much of the book, was traditionally ascribed to Solomon. That is unlikely to be the case, but it draws on the tradition of Solomon as the wise ruler of Israel (1 Kings 3:16–28; 4:20–34; 10:1–29), as a result of which he is the 'patron saint' of the Wisdom tradition.

Much of the book contains practical wisdom, to do with family life, neighbours, wealth and poverty, laziness and diligence. As you read, you will begin to recognise recurring themes. I hope that you will also enjoy the humour and vivid imagery—use your imagination to bring the pictures to life. Keep asking yourself. how does this speak to me today? Much of this ancient wisdom is still remarkably fresh and relevant.

Helen Julian CSF

Proverbs in the wild

Better is a dry morsel with quiet than a house full of feasting with strife. A slave who deals wisely will rule over a child who acts shamefully, and will share the inheritance as one of the family. The crucible is for silver, and the furnace is for gold, but the Lord tests the heart. An evildoer listens to wicked lips; and a liar gives heed to a mischievous tongue. Those who mock the poor insult their Maker; those who are glad at calamity will not go unpunished. Grandchildren are the crown of the aged, and the glory of children is their parents.

For most of the days that follow I have tried to select verses that have some themes in common, but, as we begin, here are some proverbs in their natural habitat, where each verse is separate and stands alone. These verses are a good example of the range of subject matter and approach.

Most of what is said is still good advice for today and there is little that has become outdated. Only the 'slave' in verse 2, perhaps, although, sadly, slavery is still a reality in some parts of the world.

The theme of wealth and riches is a common one throughout the book of Proverbs and our first verse here reminds us that wealth, though providing the means for feasting, does not necessarily lead to a happy and satisfying life.

Family is another common theme and our final verse expresses the importance of its continuance. To see one's grandchildren, especially when life expectancies were shorter than today, was a special blessing, guaranteeing that one's family would survive into the future.

The two verses in which God is named are interesting. As gold and silver are assayed to determine their purity, so God tests the human heart—a vivid image and not an entirely comfortable one. In verse 5, the high value of creation and, hence, of every person, is asserted in a way that seems to be original to the Israelite Wisdom literature and of which Jesus himself spoke: 'just as you did it to one of the least of these who are members of my family, you did it to me' (Matthew 25:40).

Prayer

Lord, we remember and give thanks for those who did not live to see their grandchildren, so that they might live in peace.

HJ CSF

Forgiveness and friendship

One who forgives an affront fosters friendship, but one who dwells on disputes will alienate a friend... Evil will not depart from the house of one who returns evil for good. The beginning of strife is like letting out water; so stop before the quarrel breaks out... A friend loves at all times, and kinsfolk are born to share adversity. It is senseless to give a pledge, to become surety for a neighbour.

Have you ever ignored a drip, a damp patch, only to regret it later when the situation becomes dramatically worse? 'The beginning of strife is like letting out water' is a warning about the seemingly insignificant ways in which enduring quarrels can start—just a few words or a small act of unkindness, if not dealt with immediately, can lead to a torrent that washes away friendship and perhaps much else with it.

This is not just personal, but affects whole families. The 'house' of the one who returns evil for good is not just the physical home, but the entire extended family. Those who return evil for good cannot expect others to treat them differently. Of course, the gospel demands more of us, so Jesus exhorts us to 'do good to those who hate you, bless those who curse you' (Luke 6:27—28).

The writer of Proverbs also grasped this wisdom: forgiveness is essential for friendship to flourish. He may not have been simply referring to our own relationships either. Some commentators interpret this first verse as referring also to the effect we can have on others' friendships. By our exposure of their foibles or failings, drawing attention to causes of division and not encouraging others to forgive, we can also break up their friendships. Sometimes the writer of Proverbs makes a good agony aunt!

The final verse is another place where the practical wisdom of Proverbs has been transcended by the Christian message. It is probably true that it is unwise to take the financial risk of standing surety—if surety is required, there is obviously some risk. The Christian way is to take risks for the sake of the other, for their well-being: 'For God's foolishness is wiser than human wisdom' (1 Corinthians 1:25).

Prayer

God of love, make me generous in forgiveness and in risking for others.
Amen

HJ CSF

PROVERBS 17:7–8, 15, 23, 26 (NRSV)

Power and integrity

Fine speech is not becoming to a fool; still less is false speech to a ruler. A bribe is like a magic stone in the eyes of those who give it; wherever they turn they prosper... One who justifies the wicked and one who condemns the righteous are both alike an abomination to the Lord... The wicked accept a concealed bribe to pervert the ways of justice... To impose a fine on the innocent is not right, or to flog the noble for their integrity.

You only need to read the newspaper or listen to the news to realise that, once again, the writer of Proverbs has much to say to our world. Justice and the exercise of power are still battlegrounds. Power can corrupt those who are given it—or who take it—and there will always be those who seek to gain advantage by means of their wealth and influence.

The two proverbs in today's passage that deal with bribes say rather different things, which is characteristic of this book. It is a collection of originally separate sayings, so they do not necessarily agree with each other. It probably depends on your temperament whether you find this annoying or stimulating!

The first proverb about bribes is really about the custom of offering a gift when asking a favour—normal practice in the society of the time and, indeed, in many cultures today. It is given openly and, as one commentator puts it,

'works like a charm'. The second proverb is about a different situation, that of slipping a bribe to a corrupt (or potentially corrupt) official at the right moment, so as to affect the outcome of a decision or court case. It is done in secret and intended to influence somebody with power, certainly to the advantage of the one who has given it and, perhaps, to the detriment of others.

This practice could lead to the abomination of justifying the wicked and condemning the righteous and the corruption of the legal process, which is also described in the final verse.

The integrity of those in power is a precious gift that must be nurtured and supported—that is the responsibility of us all.

Reflection

What power do you exercise? What are the temptations to misuse it?

HJ CSF

The price of wisdom

Better to meet a she-bear robbed of its cubs than to confront a fool immersed in folly... Why should fools have a price in hand to buy wisdom, when they have no mind to learn?... The one who begets a fool gets trouble; the parent of a fool has no joy... The discerning person looks to wisdom, but the eyes of a fool to the ends of the earth... Even fools who keep silent are considered wise; when they close their lips, they are deemed intelligent.

We begin today with a very vivid picture—one of the over-the-top images that the writer uses to make the point! The point is a serious one, though—those wedded to their folly are a danger not only to themselves but also others, as dangerous as a she-bear robbed of her cubs.

Foolishness and wisdom are another recurring theme in this book. The fool with 'a price in hand' is perhaps someone approaching a teacher of wisdom, seeking to learn what they have to teach. Some of the teachers may have charged fees, as do many today who claim that they can teach you things that will 'change your life'.

There are probably two points here. One is that money alone cannot make a person wise if they have no ability to learn and the other that, in any case, much wisdom cannot be 'bought' from another. Knowledge can be passed on, although even here a willing-ness to be taught is necessary, but wisdom is not just another word for knowledge. It is a deeper knowing and comes ultimately from a life lived in its pursuit.

That is what the discerning person does—keeps his or her eyes fixed on wisdom (which in the earlier chapters of Proverbs is personified as a woman), on the teacher. They concentrate on what they are being taught. The foolish, on the other hand, flit about from one thing to another, unable to concentrate, unable to make a commitment to a particular teacher and teaching. Today's technology makes it possible to know what is going on everywhere, all the time, but does this lead to wisdom? The writer of Proverbs would say that it doesn't and I'm inclined to agree.

Reflection

Am I focused on the pursuit of wisdom or the gathering of knowledge?

HJ CSF

Better together?

The one who lives alone is self-indulgent, showing contempt for all who have sound judgment. A fool takes no pleasure in understanding, but only in expressing personal opinion. When wickedness comes, contempt comes also; and with dishonour comes disgrace. The words of the mouth are deep waters; the fountain of wisdom is a gushing stream... The words of a whisperer are like delicious morsels; they go down into the inner parts of the body.

The opening of today's reading is a challenging one for a society in which more and more people live alone. Many, of course, do this not from choice, but as a result of circumstances. In the writer's day this would have been much rarer—to have lived alone would have seemed far more anti-social, a refusal to accept one's proper responsibilities to the community. His words still make a point, however. If I 'live alone' (and some can do this even while sharing their living space with others), I make my preferences, opinions and comfort paramount. Like the fool, I am not interested in understanding others, not willing to listen to them, but want only my voice to be heard and my opinions to be taken seriously.

Whether or not Anti-Social Behaviour Orders (ASBOs) are the right way to address the perceived problem, it is certainly the case that people are increasingly separated from one another, increasingly autonomous, increasingly unsure even how to relate, especially to those who are different.

In the last verse, we have a vivid picture of another destructive habit. Gossip is big business and there seems an insatiable appetite for 'delicious morsels' about celebrities. Perhaps much of this is harmless, but when it comes closer to home it can be hugely destructive. There is something in human nature that loves to know a secret, something others don't know, but, like food, when it is taken in, it becomes part of us and affects who we are.

Such words stand in sharp contrast to the 'fountain of wisdom', the deep words of wisdom, the words of life. Initially they may be less tempting, but they nourish us in healthier ways and perhaps help to make us more open to the world around us and the needs of others.

Reflection

Which do I choose—delicious morsels or the fountain of wisdom?

HJ CSF

Trust me

The name of the Lord is a strong tower; the righteous run into it and are safe. The wealth of the rich is their strong city; in their imagination it is like a high wall. Before destruction one's heart is haughty, but humility goes before honour... The human spirit will endure sickness; but a broken spirit—who can bear? An intelligent mind acquires knowledge, and the ear of the wise seeks knowledge.

Trust is a valuable commodity. Polls explore which professions are most and least trusted; companies produce advertisements selling the idea that we can trust them with our money, health or safety. The abuse of trust is one of the hardest things to forgive.

The first two proverbs today address this question: where do we put our trust? The second proverb is in itself quite neutral. Those who have plenty of money (and in this culture wealth was seen as a gift from God) have the security of a high wall around them. The first proverb, however, points to a contrast. The righteous have a different source of security—the name of the Lord. 'The name of the Lord' often refers to some particular aspect of God's nature—here it is about God's power to protect.

When I think of 'a strong tower', I remember the pele towers in the borderlands between Scotland and England, to which people could retreat with their livestock when raiders came. They had only one entrance, above ground level, and, once the people had all come inside, the ladder would be drawn up. The animals had to live a little more dangerously at ground level! I find it a powerful image of God's protective power, a power that can be trusted.

The writer here shows an acute insight into sickness and health. If our spirit is sound, we can live with physical illness. In fact, many people with severe limitations manage to live with grace and a large measure of freedom. We may also know people, though, who have allowed illness, disability, difficulty and so on to shape their lives and narrow them down. We may have struggled with these questions ourselves. Perhaps putting our trust in God can be a way out of such situations and into a place of greater freedom.

Reflection

'In you O Lord I put my trust.' Do I?

HJ CSF

PROVERBS 19:2–3, 21, 23, 27 (NRSV)

Tightropes and pitfalls

Desire without knowledge is not good, and one who moves too hurriedly misses the way. One's own folly leads to ruin, yet the heart rages against the Lord... The human mind may devise many plans, but it is the purpose of the Lord that will be established... The fear of the Lord is life indeed; filled with it one rests secure and suffers no harm... Cease straying, my child, from the words of knowledge, in order that you may hear instruction.

Today's proverbs lead us out on to a tightrope. The writer constantly exhorts his readers to be wise, seek understanding, hear instruction. There is always another dimension, though—God's will, purpose and plans. This dichotomy has often been a pitfall (to mix metaphors) for Christians. The temptation is to come down on one side or the other: God has a plan for my life and all I can do is pray for it to be revealed to me. Until that happens, I can make no decisions. The alternative is to think that God has given me a mind for a purpose. I can investigate all the possibilities, weigh up the options and come to a decision.

The reality is that we need to step out on to the tightrope. On the one hand is the wisdom that is God's gift, to be acquired through effort and perseverance. On the other is 'the purpose of the Lord' and, ultimately, it is the purpose of all our knowledge and wisdom to see better how to align ourselves with God's purposes for ourselves and our world.

The writer has some useful advice for us as we wobble out on to the tightrope. It is right to take time to reflect, not to rush into action on the basis of what we desire. We might find ourselves heading off in the wrong direction. If we choose our direction on the basis of our own foolishness (that is, our minds and hearts without reference to God), then we must not blame God if things don't turn out as we'd hoped.

The proper 'fear' of God (perhaps 'respect' is a more appropriate word today) will give us the life that is life indeed and a security that rests on more than our own knowing.

Reflection

On which side of the dichotomy do you naturally fall?

HJ CSF

PROVERBS 19:7, 13–14, 18, 26 (NRSV)

The gift of family

If the poor are hated even by their kin, how much more are they shunned by their friends! When they call after them, they are not there... A stupid child is ruin to a father, and a wife's quarrelling is a continual dripping of rain. House and wealth are inherited from parents, but a prudent wife is from the Lord... Discipline your children while there is hope; do not set your heart on their destruction... Those who do violence to their father and chase away their mother are children who cause shame and bring reproach.

Do you remember the small drip of water that, if not dealt with, can destroy friendship? Here is the same image, but this time it is more akin to Chinese water torture. The literal translation speaks of a leak that harries or pursues. This time, the context is the family—another major theme of the book of Proverbs.

A quarrelsome member of the family (and not just a wife), someone who is always finding fault, picking on others, can be as damaging as a constantly dripping gutter, wearing away at whatever it comes into contact with. Our closest relations can also be those who can do us the most damage—they have the opportunity and they know our weak points.

They can also be God's gift to us. Inheritance may be anticipated, but the people with whom we choose to share our life, build our own family, cannot. We can probably all remember daydream-ing about our perfect partner, the handsome man or beautiful woman who would sweep us off our feet and transform our lives. The real person when he or she appears in our lives is usually very different. Can we appreciate them as the gift that they are?

The first proverb, odd though this may seem, actually speaks of the strength of family. Those in need may be shunned by their friends, but, although families may struggle with those who make demands, far fewer will cut off the needy member and refuse to hear his or her cry for help. Many families struggle on heroically, caring for a disabled child, a chronically ill spouse, an ageing parent. They do not reject the gift of God.

Prayer

Today, pray for your family, giving thanks for this gift from God.

HJ CSF

Knowing ourselves?

The purposes in the human mind are like deep water, but the intelligent will draw them out… A king who sits on the throne of judgment winnows all evil with his eyes. Who can say, 'I have made my heart clean; I am pure from my sin?'… Even children make themselves known by their acts, by whether what they do is pure and right. The hearing ear and the seeing eye—the Lord has made them both… All our steps are ordered by the Lord; how then can we understand our own ways?… The human spirit is the lamp of the Lord, searching every innermost part.

Today's theme is self-knowledge and, as we have seen elsewhere, there are, even within these few verses, differing perspectives.

There is the hopeful: we can know ourselves, with God's help. Our senses—the hearing ear and the seeing eye—have been made by God and so they are of good quality. The maker's name guarantees their reliability. More profoundly, we have God's spirit within us. The final proverb is literally translated 'The breath of man is Yahweh's lamp', linking the giving of breath at creation, God breathing his own life into us, with the inner light, the inner sense of right and wrong that can guide us to know ourselves better and understand our motives.

Then there is the evidence of our actions. 'Actions speak louder than words', runs one of our own proverbs and the writer here sees this as innate, operating from our earliest years. If you want to know what you really care about, look for what you spend your time, energy and money on. Most people, when they see a discrepancy between another's words and their actions will believe the actions rather than the words.

Then there is our frequent puzzlement about our own and others' actions and words. We may think that we are doing the right thing, but how can we be sure that our heart is clean and our motives are right? We find ourselves doing what we don't want to do and not doing what we do want to do (Romans 7:19)—how can we understand our own ways? These are deep waters indeed and we need both intelligence and God's guidance to really know ourselves and others.

Prayer

Lord, give me your lamp, to know myself better.

HJ CSF

PROVERBS 20:4, 10, 13–14, 17 (NRSV)

Uncomfortable truths

The lazy person does not plough in season; harvest comes, and there is nothing to be found... Diverse weights and diverse measures are both alike an abomination to the Lord... Do not love sleep, or else you will come to poverty; open your eyes, and you will have plenty of bread. 'Bad, bad,' says the buyer, then goes away and boasts... Bread gained by deceit is sweet, but afterward the mouth will be full of gravel.

Laziness and deceit are not comfortable topics to consider, but they are part of human life and, as such, find a place in this book of practical wisdom.

The condemnation of deceit is a good reminder that, in God's economy, our knowledge, and even our wisdom, are not to be used in sharp practice, cheating others or devising clever schemes to part the foolish from their money.

The condemnation of diverse weights and measures—in other words, weights and measures that change depending on the customer or perhaps according to whether their owner is buying or selling—is deeply rooted in the Old Testament. Deuteronomy 25:13–16 contains the law on this topic. It was obviously not observed by all, however, because later we find that the prophets are still condemning the practice (Amos 8:5; Micah 6:11). Today's equivalent might perhaps be the comfortable financial deals available to the better off, while the

poor pay high interest or cannot get credit at all.

The picture of the buyer saying 'bad, bad' and then going away to boast of having got a good deal is not necessarily deceitful, but reflects the haggling of a society with no fixed prices. The writer warns that if such rituals between buyer and seller become deceitful, what is gained by it will become unpalatable. The initial sweetness will become gritty and unpleasant.

Perhaps laziness is also a form of deceit. Those who could be earning their own living, but who choose instead to rely on others, are living a life that is not true. Perhaps, more deeply, they are deceiving themselves, not using their abilities or their creativity. Bread gained by one's own effort is more likely to taste good.

Reflection

Where do you see laziness or deceit operating in your own life or society?

HJ CSF

PROVERBS 20:1–2, 15, 21, 29 (NRSV)

Using God's gifts wisely

Wine is a mocker, strong drink a brawler, and whoever is led astray by it is not wise. The dread anger of a king is like the growling of a lion; anyone who provokes him to anger forfeits life itself... There is gold, and abundance of costly stones, but the lips informed by knowledge are a precious jewel... An estate quickly acquired in the beginning will not be blessed in the end... The glory of youths is their strength, but the beauty of the aged is their grey hair.

Our proverb writer has a gift for the striking image and the telling phrase. As so often, even though he uses images from his own time and culture, many of them are relevant to our lives today. Only a little translation is needed.

Alcohol as a 'mocker' and a 'brawler'—many of our city centres on a Saturday night bear witness to the accuracy of these vivid personifications of 'wine' and 'strong drink'. Once again, the consequences of overindulgence are described in terms of being wise or foolish. Like all of God's gifts, alcohol is meant to be a pleasure, but when it takes the lead and the drinker surrenders control, it is easy to be led astray, into behaviour that is foolish or a lot worse.

Wealth is another of God's gifts and is not to be despised, but it is less desirable than 'lips informed by knowledge'—perhaps a way of saying that intelligent advice has a price above gold or precious stones.

The king was the holder of ultimate power and his anger, like that of a lion, could be lethal. In many parts of the world this is still the case—power is absolute. It's a reminder to be grateful for the checks and balances in the exercise of power that most of us enjoy.

Sudden riches have their perils, too, even if honestly gained, although some commentators think that this verse may refer to seizing an inheritance prematurely (we may be reminded of the parable of the prodigal son). That action is one of disrespect to the aged, which is very much at odds with the society of Proverbs' time. The young will always be valued for their youth, but how much do we value grey hair today?

Prayer

*Generous God, may I use your gifts
with wisdom today.*

HJ CSF

My heart is in God's hands

The king's heart is a stream of water in the hand of the Lord; he turns it wherever he will. All deeds are right in the sight of the doer, but the Lord weighs the heart. To do righteousness and justice is more acceptable to the Lord than sacrifice... Whoever pursues righteousness and kindness will find life and honour... No wisdom, no understanding no counsel, can avail against the Lord. The horse is made ready for the day of battle, but the victory belongs to the Lord.

The king in Israel was seen as having been appointed and anointed by God and therefore having a special relationship of closeness to God. The image of the king's heart as a stream of water in God's hand stems from this understanding. We should remember, too, that the heart was considered not just the place of emotions as it is for us but also the centre of intellectual and moral life. In 2:2, the writer of Proverbs encourages his reader to incline 'your heart to understanding'—we would more naturally say 'your mind' here. The image in 21:1 is that of a farmer guiding water along irrigation channels in his fields, leading it to where it is needed.

The picture of God weighing the heart may have been influenced by the Egyptian belief that the human heart was weighed after death to see whether or not during life it had conformed to 'truth'. It is in any case a striking image, introducing in these proverbs the idea that, however hard we try to judge our own actions and motivations, only God can, in the end, make the true judgment. This shows some development on the older Wisdom tradition, where wisdom could be pursued and found by human effort—the king was guided by wise counsellors, acting as a kind of 'cabinet'. Here, there is movement towards the idea, found in the prophets, that only God has true wisdom and all human wisdom and judgment must submit to him.

Sacrifice is also relativised. It is not considered wrong, but other things, 'righteousness and justice', are more important—another insight from the prophets.

Finally, we are reminded that neither armed might nor diplomatic alliances can necessarily prevail. The horse may be ready, but victory and defeat are in God's hands.

Reflection

Does God have control of your 'heart'?

HJ CSF

PROVERBS 21:6–7, 10, 12–13, 26, 29 (NRSV)

The world cries out

The getting of treasures by a lying tongue is a fleeting vapour and a snare of death. The violence of the wicked will sweep them away, because they refuse to do what is just... The souls of the wicked desire evil; their neighbours find no mercy in their eyes... The Righteous One observes the house of the wicked; he casts the wicked down to ruin. If you close your ear to the cry of the poor, you will cry out and not be heard... All day long the wicked covet, but the righteous give and do not hold back... The wicked put on a bold face, but the upright give thought to their ways.

Does anyone read *The Water Babies* by Charles Kingsley today? I can remember it from my childhood, although it wasn't one of my favourites. I think even then I found the moralising a bit heavy-handed. Kingsley wasn't subtle—with a character called 'Mrs Do-as you-would-be-done-by' his message was pretty clear.

Our proverb writer has the same clear message. If you do not listen and respond to those in need when you could offer help, then, in your time of need, you must not expect your cry to be heard.

That is not just neglect, but a positive choice to not do what is right. It's interesting that the writer names this as 'violence'. In our day, the whole world is our neighbour and the call to show mercy, hear the cry of the poor is thus far more pressing and far more overwhelming. We can feel swamped by the needs of the world and retreat into our own little world, closing our eyes and our ears.

Perhaps the remedy is to be found in verse 26: 'All day long the wicked covet, but the righteous give and do not hold back.' Commentators find this hard to interpret, but I agree with one who sees it as making a contrast between those whose lives are daily shaped by their own desires and those who look outside and give generously from whatever they have. It is perhaps a difference in the centre of gravity, between the key pronoun being 'I' or 'we'.

Reflection

Where is my centre of gravity? Dare I open my eyes and ears to the cries of the world?

HJ CSF

Miscellaneous soundbites

The eyes of the Lord keep watch over knowledge, but he overthrows the words of the faithless. The lazy person says, 'There is a lion outside! I shall be killed in the streets!' The mouth of a loose woman is a deep pit; he with whom the Lord is angry falls into it. Folly is bound up in the heart of a boy, but the rod of discipline drives it far away. Oppressing the poor in order to enrich oneself, and giving to the rich, will lead only to loss.

To finish our journey through this section of Proverbs, I've again chosen a few continuous verses—proverbs in their natural habitat. The wonderfully random nature of the subjects and the advice given is a good reminder of the 'sound-bite' quality of most of this book and how we need to read it.

We have the primacy of God, keeping watch over knowledge and, we can assume from other proverbs, over the wise, but overthrowing the faithless and the foolish. It is in God's power to judge between the two.

Then there is another wonderfully over-the-top description of laziness, as desperate and unbelievable as the best reasons for not handing in one's homework at school! A lion in the street definitely trumps a mere dog.

With the 'loose woman' we see one of the more difficult aspects of our proverb writer: the tendency to use this particular image as a picture of the dangers awaiting those who go astray. It is very much of its culture and its time, so is hard for us to use today. Perhaps if we see it as a warning against unfaithfulness, against the 'adultery' that breaks promises and covenants, it can still teach us something, even if we wouldn't use this image.

The 'rod of discipline' is another problematic phrase. The place of physical punishment in bringing up children has changed dramatically over the last 50 years, let alone since the time of Proverbs. There is still a recognition, though, of the need for boundaries so that children feel safe.

Finally, there is the recognition that how we treat others in our society is also of concern to God and affects our own well-being.

Reflection

What is your favourite proverb from this fortnight? How will you put it into practice?

HJ CSF

Christ the King

If the prevailing use of the contemporary version of the Lord's Prayer is an indicator, we think more in terms of place and less in terms of kingdom than we used to. Previous generations prayed for God's will to be done *in* earth (in the kingdom of earth), whereas our own generation prays for his will to be done *in* the kingdom of heaven, but *on* earth (the place). The change from *in* to *on* reflects a shift in our thinking as we now tend to think of God's kingdom spreading on earth, rather than the earth being a kingdom in its own right (with God as its king). If we are not careful, this leads us to regard the kingdom of God as a purely 'spiritual' realm, which may then lead us to ignore 'earthly' issues of justice, oppression and need, while we concentrate, instead, on 'spiritual' issues (to be, as they say, 'so heavenly minded that we are of no earthly use'). If, however, we believe that our world could be one kingdom under one king (Jesus) and his will could be done *in* earth, we may be more ready to apply our faith in social action.

Well, be that as it may, whether we say in or on, Christ is the King and, for the next two weeks, we shall be thinking about what kind of king he is, what kind of kingdom he rules over. We'll think about what it means for Jesus to sit on the throne of David and rule over the house of Jacob, for him to occupy this throne and his people to be 'kingdom people'.

Before we begin, we should consider one foundational truth. As we think about thrones and kings, we should remember that God's throne and God's kingship existed before creation and will last into eternity. All human thrones, kings and kingdoms are temporary and their power belongs only to the kingdom of earth. As we focus on the kingship of Jesus, we shall be looking at a divine ordinance and a throne that is, by definition, 'divine'. Our contemporary culture may interpret this as 'spiritual' and, therefore, disconnected from daily life (or even 'fictional' and therefore safely ignored), but, according to the Bible, Christ's kingdom and throne are the only ones that affect every human being and they will never pass away, ever.

David Robertson

LUKE 1:28, 30–33 (NIV, ABRIDGED)

How can this be?

The angel went to [Mary] and said, 'Greetings, you who are highly favoured! The Lord is with you... Do not be afraid, Mary, you have found favour with God. You will be with child and give birth to a son, and you are to give him the name Jesus. He will be great and will be called the Son of the Most High. The Lord God will give him the throne of his father David, and he will reign over the house of Jacob for ever; his kingdom will never end.'

This passage may be so familiar to us that we fail to notice an obvious question. How could Jesus be a king? Mary lived in Nazareth and, even if she was distantly related to David, she wasn't a queen herself, so how could her baby be royal? We can answer this question in two ways.

First of all, we know from verse 35 that the Holy Spirit will 'father' this child and he will be called the Son of God. That's about as royal a lineage as it is possible to claim! Second, the angel could have said that Jesus would sit on the throne of Solomon or even Herod and would reign over the people of Israel, but he didn't. He said that he would occupy the throne of David and reign over the house of Jacob. Why? This is a message direct from God, so we should reflect on its meaning.

God holds Mary in high favour, but he also knows that no child of hers will have royal credentials. Solomon did, as did Herod, but David didn't. He was chosen by God to replace the existing king, Saul (see 1 Samuel 15 and 16). That Mary's child will sit on the throne of David is not only the prophetic fulfilment of his lineage, but also a confirmation of his lack of it, in earthly terms! Jesus, like David, will be given his throne by God, anointed by God for the task and, like David, he will be directly, inseparably, dependant on God.

What will he rule—a country? No—Jacob was the father of the twelve tribes when the Hebrew nation was a nomadic family. On this Sunday of Christ the King, we remember that Jesus will reign over people, God's people, wherever they are.

Prayer

Lord Jesus, be my king.

DR

Make room, make room!

After Jesus was born in Bethlehem in Judea, during the time of King Herod, Magi from the east came to Jerusalem and asked, 'Where is the one who has been born king of the Jews? We saw his star in the east and have come to worship him.' When King Herod heard this he was disturbed, and all Jerusalem with him. When he had called together all the people's chief priests and teachers of the law, he asked them where the Christ was to be born. 'In Bethlehem in Judea', they replied.

I suspect that my infant school's idea of Christmas was more informed by carols than the Bible, so, at the age of six, I was one of 'three kings' in our nativity play, although the Gospels make no mention of kings, just 'magi'. Whether they were astrologers, wise men or even 'kings' of some kind, they knew that a king had been born in Israel and made a beeline for the obvious place: the palace. They probably expected Herod, the proud father, to usher them into the royal nursery. In reality, they had made a fatal mistake. The repercussions were murderous. No wonder Jerusalem was 'disturbed' as well as Herod.

There is, however, a startling irony here. The magi—visitors from another land and another religion—welcomed the arrival of the new king. In fact, if verse 16's mention of 'boys… two years old and under' is to be understood as the time between their first sight-ing of the star and their arrival in Jerusalem, they committed a number of years to this journey. By contrast, Herod, ruler of God's people, utterly rejected the new king—and not out of ignorance. He called on his religious advisers to search the scriptures and tell him exactly where the Messiah would be born. He then used that information to guide the murder of innocent children. The magi and Herod alike understood what God had done; the difference between them was that, unlike Herod, the magi were content to accept a new king.

It's easy to judge, but Jesus says that we shouldn't (Luke 6:37). In a way, we are all kings or queens of our own lives, so we all have a decision to make. Will we welcome the new king?

Reflection

When Jesus is king of my life, I'm not.

DR

Born to be my king

When Jesus saw Nathanael approaching, he said of him, 'Here is a true Israelite, in whom there is nothing false.' 'How do you know me?' Nathanael asked. Jesus answered, 'I saw you while you were still under the fig-tree before Philip called you.' Then Nathanael declared, 'Rabbi, you are the Son of God; you are the King of Israel.' Jesus said, 'You believe because I told you I saw you under the fig-tree. You shall see greater things than that.' He then added, 'I tell you the truth, you shall see heaven open, and the angels of God ascending and descending on the Son of Man.'

We meet Nathanael twice in the Gospel of John. Here, at the beginning of Jesus' ministry, and again at the new beginning of Jesus' resurrection (John 21:2). We can presume that he was there whenever the twelve disciples are mentioned, but nothing else is specifically recorded about him. We know nothing of his successes or failures or what he said and did, which means that we have no idea whether or not this conversation was typical of Nathanael or a one-off.

What we do know is that when Jesus first met him, he declared Nathanael to be straight as a die, as we might say, and Nathanael reacted to this assertion with a leap of faith. We can only speculate about what Nathanael was thinking as he sat under that tree, but, when Jesus complimented him, he had a sense of being known.

I guess we have all had that experience. We may meet someone and, after only a short time, feel that we have known them all our lives. More than that, though, there are times when we are aware of God's scrutiny, the sense that he is looking at us and knows us. For Nathanael, it seems that his first meeting with Jesus was just such a moment.

In a way, Nathanael's leap of faith was a leap of logic. If Jesus was indeed the Son of God, then he was, by default, also Israel's king. Nathanael's declaration, though, is more than a statement of objective fact. There's a sense that Nathanael not only recognises *the* king, but *his* king. It's a life-changing moment of recognition, humility and acceptance that many of us will feel echoes our own experiences.

Prayer
Lord, you know me; you are my king.

DR

Actions speak louder than words

Jesus then took the loaves, gave thanks, and distributed to those who were seated as much as they wanted. He did the same with the fish. When they had all had enough to eat, he said to his disciples, 'Gather the pieces that are left over. Let nothing be wasted.' So they gathered them and filled twelve baskets with the pieces of the five barley loaves left over by those who had eaten. After the people saw the miraculous sign that Jesus did, they began to say, 'Surely this is the Prophet who is to come into the world.' Jesus, knowing that they intended to come and make him king by force, withdrew again to a mountain by himself.

In our multicultural world, we are used to the idea that different cultures hold different values and those values inform behaviour. In Jesus' time, the culture of his homeland was not so much multicultural as bicultural, with conflicting Roman and Hebrew values. Today's reading is quintessentially Hebrew.

In our culture, how would we react to a miracle like this? Being used to media magicians such as David Blaine and Derren Brown, many would, no doubt, be intrigued and wonder how it was done. In Jesus' day, the crowd wanted to march him off to Jerusalem and declare him king. That is because they reacted according to their value system. The Romans, like the Greeks, regarded argument, reason and explanation as the proof of something, so they (like most of us) would have wanted to discuss the miracle to determine whether or not it had really happened and, if it had,

what it meant. The Hebrew mindset, though, regarded action as proof, so, by performing this miracle, Jesus had proved his words (see 1 Corinthians 1:22). More specifically, by feeding the crowd, Jesus had demonstrated God's power, so the only reasonable course of action was to recognise God's chosen man—Jesus—as king.

Jesus, however, withdrew before the march could begin because his kingship is not man-made. He occupies the throne of David and reigns over the house of Jacob at God's command, not by human election. In this sense, none of us 'enthrones' Jesus—he is king regardless of our opinions or behaviour. He is enthroned over all people and reigns over every culture.

Reflection

'At the name of Jesus, every knee should bow' (Philippians 2:10).

DR

MATTHEW 20:20–23 (NIV)

Be careful what you wish for

Then the mother of Zebedee's sons came to Jesus with her sons and, kneeling down, asked a favour of him. 'What is it you want?' he asked. She said, 'Grant that one of these two sons of mine may sit at your right and the other at your left in your kingdom.' 'You don't know what you are asking,' Jesus said to them. 'Can you drink the cup I am going to drink?' 'We can', they answered. Jesus said to them, 'You will indeed drink from my cup, but to sit at my right or left is not for me to grant. These places belong to those for whom they have been prepared by my Father.'

When I was in my mid-30s I found out that my school had not intended to enter me for any O level exams. Apparently, my teachers didn't think it worthwhile and they relented only when my parents interceded on my behalf. I knew nothing of this—I just turned up, passed them all, did my A levels and went on to university. My parents did not mention it for 20 years. That's what parents do. Here, James' and John's mum intercedes on behalf of her sons. After all, they'd given up the family business to follow Jesus (Luke 5:10–11), so shouldn't they receive a reward?

The trouble is, when it comes to Jesus' kingdom, the question, 'What's in it for me?' has a straightforward answer: the same as what was in it for Jesus! If the cross is the gateway to Jesus' kingdom, anyone following him will have to travel the same route.

Without realising it, Mrs Zebedee was asking if her sons might be crucified with their king and, in their case, Jesus' answer was 'Yes' for both of them.

If death is the gateway to Jesus' kingdom, what of life in eternity? As Jesus says, who will be at his right and left side is the Father's decision, but he does make a promise to his disciples on another occasion: 'And I confer on you a kingdom, just as my Father conferred one on me, so that you may eat and drink at my table in my kingdom and sit on thrones, judging the twelve tribes of Israel' (Luke 22:29–30).

Prayer

Lord, give me strength to take up my own cross, daily, and follow you.

DR

Every king has a throne

Then the whole assembly rose and led [Jesus] off to Pilate. And they began to accuse him, saying, 'We have found this man subverting our nation. He opposes payment of taxes to Caesar and claims to be Christ, a king.' So Pilate asked Jesus, 'Are you the king of the Jews?' 'Yes, it is as you say', Jesus replied. Then Pilate announced to the chief priests and the crowd, 'I find no basis for a charge against this man'... The soldiers also came up and mocked him. They offered him wine vinegar and said, 'If you are the king of the Jews, save yourself.' There was a written notice above him, which read: THIS IS THE KING OF THE JEWS.

Had Herod (the Great) still been alive, he would no doubt have closed the 'Jesus case file' with some relief at this point. What began with the visit of the magi was finally finished, now that the upstart king was executed.

For Pilate, this was not a straightforward matter. When he met Jesus and talked to him, he saw no reason to charge him. Whether he thought that Jesus was well meaning but misguided or he considered him to be mad we have no idea. One thing is obvious: Jesus was neither a brother of Herod (the Tetrarch) nor the son of any other king and, even if he had been, his crown would have needed the approval of Caesar. Jesus was just a man from Nazareth and, clearly, he wasn't a king! In fact, Jesus was a nobody and Pilate could do what he liked with him—and he did.

As Jesus was handed over for scourging and then crucifixion, reality and theology merge. Jesus, the ultimate somebody who became a nobody, laid down his life that everybody might become a somebody in the kingdom of God (Philippians 2:6–8). Pilate, probably as an insult to the religious leaders in Jerusalem, insisted that Jesus die for the crime with which he was charged and had a notice to that effect nailed above his head.

That notice was wrong. It should have read: 'This is the king', full stop. Jesus was—is—the king of everyone, everywhere, for all time.

Reflection

The cross is the earthly throne of this King.

DR

The power and the glory

Then Jesus asked, 'What is the kingdom of God like? What shall I compare it to? It is like a mustard seed, which a man took and planted in his garden. It grew and became a tree, and the birds of the air perched in its branches.' Again he asked, 'What shall I compare the kingdom of God to? It is like yeast that a woman took and mixed into a large amount of flour until it worked all through the dough.'

When Jesus met Pilate, he admitted that he was a king, but he also declared that his kingdom was 'not of this world' (John 18:36). That was why he refused to allow the enthusiastic crowd to march him off to Jerusalem (as we saw in Wednesday's reading)—he would not be a king in that way. He did, however, travel to Jerusalem and give himself up to crucifixion—as a king (as we saw yesterday).

We could compare earthly kingdom after kingdom and they would all be either subtly or obviously different from one another. Does Jesus' kingdom bear a resemblance to any of those kingdoms? No. His kingdom looks unlike any other kingdom. It starts small but grows into a place of refuge, like the mustard tree. It is like yeast—a tiny, quiet thing working to change everything. When you see a tree, you don't think about the seed; when you see bread, you don't think about the yeast. Jesus may sit on the throne of David, but, when you look at his kingdom, you may not, at first, see the king. Rather, you will see those who belong to the kingdom, those in whom the king has planted the seed of his word, who have been infused with the yeast of his Spirit.

There are those who think that the kingdom of God should, like a powerful wind, blow all before it. Others think that the kingdom ought to shake the world to its core, like an earthquake. There are still others who see it as a sweeping, cleansing fire. Jesus' description in today's reading is of his kingdom being more like a quiet whisper, which shouldn't surprise us. After all, God doesn't change (see 1 Kings 19:11–12 for the story of Elijah and the quietness of God).

Reflection

What does it mean to be 'a kingdom person'?

DR

JOHN 12:12–16 (NIV)

The shout and the whisper

The next day the great crowd that had come for the Feast heard that Jesus was on his way to Jerusalem. They took palm branches and went out to meet him, shouting, 'Hosanna!' 'Blessed is he who comes in the name of the Lord!' 'Blessed is the King of Israel!' Jesus found a young donkey and sat upon it, as it is written, 'Do not be afraid, O Daughter of Zion; see, your king is coming, seated on a donkey's colt.' At first his disciples did not understand all this. Only after Jesus was glorified did they realise that these things had been written about him and that they had done these things to him.

Today, Advent Sunday, we begin a new church season and prepare for the arrival of the king. We prepare for Christmas (the first coming of Jesus) and also look ahead to his second coming and ask this question: 'Are we ready?'

To begin this new season, I've chosen a reading that describes what happened when Jesus was publically welcomed as the king of Israel. When the king arrived, there were those who were ready for him and those who were not.

Initially, the crowd went wild and people were inspired to shout out and prepare the way with 'banners', while their acclaimed king rode into their capital city. The king was here! His kingdom had come! It was all amazing!

What exactly does this mean? The disciples, to name just 12 of those present, had no idea and neither did the crowd, actually. Within days they would change

their tune and bay for Jesus' blood (Luke 23:18), yet here, indeed, were both the king and the kingdom. The words of welcome were accurate enough, but words are just words and they had not lodged in the lives of those who shouted them.

The disciples, however, had had the mustard seeds of the words planted in their minds. Later, when the yeast of God's Spirit dwelt within them (see Matthew 13:31–33), their understanding grew into a great truth: Jesus was—and is—the king.

His kingdom was not seen in the power of the crowd; it was seen in the personal whisper heard, but as yet not understood, by the disciples.

Prayer

Lord, grow your kingdom in me.

DR

One shall tell another

As his custom was, Paul went into the synagogue, and on three Sabbath days he reasoned with them from the Scriptures... But the Jews were jealous; so they rounded up some bad characters from the marketplace, formed a mob and started a riot in the city. They rushed to Jason's house in search of Paul and Silas in order to bring them out to the crowd. But when they did not find them, they dragged Jason and some other believers before the city officials, shouting: 'These people who have caused trouble all over the world have now come here, and Jason has welcomed them into his house. They are all defying Caesar's decrees, saying that there is another king, one called Jesus.'

I find it very hard to read the names of Paul and Silas without tapping my foot. As a teenager I abandoned the ukulele in favour of bluegrass banjo and one of the first songs I learned was 'Gimme that old time religion'. The only line I now remember is, 'It was good for Paul and Silas and it's good enough for me', but my foot still taps on cue. Years after learning this song, it struck me that it describes how the mustard seed, the kingdom of God, grows and spreads.

When Paul arrived in Thessalonica, he spent time in the synagogue discussing Jesus with anyone who would listen—and Jason was among them. As Paul explained the scriptures, proving that Jesus was the Messiah and showing why he died and rose again (v. 3), the seed of God's word was planted in Jason. The Spirit evidently nurtured his faith and he must have spoken to others about his new king, Jesus. Using this against him, the leaders of the synagogue hauled him off to the authorities, where he was fined (v. 9).

Jason was a member of the synagogue before he met Paul and Silas. He already believed in God and knew the scriptures, but to meet Jesus the king he needed to meet kingdom people. To misquote the song, 'It was good for Paul and Silas and it was good enough for Jason!' I echo the same process in my own Christian history, but I would say, 'Keith and John'—the kingdom people who made an impact on me.

Prayer

*Lord, may I too be a sower
of your words.*

DR

The throne of David

Jesus said to them, 'I tell you the truth, at the renewal of all things, when the Son of Man sits on his glorious throne, you who have followed me will also sit on twelve thrones, judging the twelve tribes of Israel. And everyone who has left houses or brothers or sisters or father or mother or children or fields for my sake will receive a hundred times as much and will inherit eternal life. But many who are first will be last, and many who are last will be first.'

In our culture, the thought of our queen sitting on her throne tends to conjure up images of pomp and pageantry. Historically, a monarch's throne was the place from which they made laws and delivered judgments. Even when there was a legal system, it was the king who made the laws and who was the final judge in difficult cases. In the Bible, the early kings were required to act in this way, too (for example, Solomon in 1 Kings 3:16–28), and this persisted into Jesus' time (for example, when Paul, disgruntled with the legal process, appealed directly to Caesar in Acts 25:11).

In our culture, even though our queen approves legislation, it is the House of Commons that makes laws and the House of Lords acts as the final court of appeal. To us, then, this ancient posture (sitting on a throne) means little. It's more a sign of solemnity and ceremony than the making of laws or judgments that will affect our lives. If we are not careful, that is how we also see the throne of Jesus: as a glorious statement of his kingship, but with little practical application. In the New Testament, though, whenever Jesus' throne is referred to, it has a direct meaning. This is where the king sits to judge and his word is law. If he rules in our favour, we shall have life more abundantly than we expect or deserve.

In today's reading, Jesus paints a picture similar to that of an earthly king rewarding his military leaders after a hard-fought campaign (with titles, land and wealth), but then the image changes. When Jesus rules, it's not necessarily the obvious people who are rewarded and, actually, there is only one reward—eternal life.

Prayer
Thank you, Lord, for your promise of eternal life.

DR

Kingly authority

Some men came carrying a paralytic on a mat... they went up on the roof and lowered him on his mat through the tiles into the middle of the crowd, right in front of Jesus. When Jesus saw their faith, he said, 'Friend, your sins are forgiven.' The Pharisees and the teachers of the law began thinking to themselves, 'Who is this fellow who speaks blasphemy? Who can forgive sins but God alone?' Jesus knew what they were thinking... He said to the paralysed man, 'I tell you, get up, take your mat and go home.' Immediately he stood up in front of them, took what he had been lying on and went home praising God.

In today's reading we see a good example of the double aspect of the throne of David. The first of these is as a throne of law. On this occasion, a paralysed man is brought to Jesus and Jesus absolves him of sin. This absolution is a word of divine law and, as the Pharisees and teachers of law quickly spot, it is a word that can be spoken only by the one who occupies the throne of God. By declaring the man free from sin, Jesus is, they think, usurping the place of God, which, for a human being, is blasphemy.

Jesus responds by delivering another word from the throne of law. This time it is a declaration of physical freedom as he tells the man to get up and walk home. Now his critics are silenced because, to their way of thinking, the miracle proves Jesus' word of absolution (if the man is walking, he must also be forgiven) and everyone is amazed (v. 26).

There are other, similar, occasions when people are amazed by Jesus' words and deeds (for example Luke 4:36) and they often express their shock by questioning his 'authority'. They don't understand where he gets this authority from, but we do. It comes from occupying the throne of law.

Second, as we saw yesterday, this throne is a throne of judgment. As Jesus speaks 'law', everyone reacts. Some rejoice and praise God; others reject him and plan to get rid of him. What no one understands at the time is that, as they judge Jesus, they are judging the one who will judge them.

Reflection

Jesus' throne of judgment, like his kingdom, is not of this world.

DR

The heavenly host

[Jesus said to his disciples] 'When the Son of Man comes in his glory, and all the angels with him, he will sit on his throne in heavenly glory. All the nations will be gathered before him, and he will separate the people one from another as a shepherd separates the sheep from the goats. He will put the sheep on his right and the goats on his left. Then the King will say to those on his right, "Come, you who are blessed by my Father; take your inheritance, the kingdom prepared for you since the creation of the world."'

As we have already established, Jesus' throne is a throne of law and judgment, just as the thrones of past were. Even then, however, being a king was about more than just sitting on the throne as a sign of authority. In those days, the king also led the army and went into battle with his troops, often leading from the front. So, if Jesus is a king, does he have an army? Yes, he does, which is the picture painted in today's passage. It is a description of the 'day of judgment' when the king is flanked by not just a couple of angels, but by *all* of the angels.

If our thinking about angels has been formed largely by stained glass windows and Christmas cards, we probably think of them as a kind of heavenly choir. According to the Bible, angels do more than sing. They carry messages (as we saw in our first reading in this series), but they also behave as 'heavenly troops'. For example, it was angels who fought for Elisha (2 Kings 6:16–18) and angels who will be instrumental at the final judgment (Revelation 15). When Jesus speaks of his second coming, angels are not included in the picture as a heavenly choir, but as the army of the king.

In recent years, this strand of biblical teaching has been sensationalised and there has been a stream of novels and films depicting warrior angels. In actual fact, it makes no difference to human beings whether angels are choristers or stormtroopers. Whether they sing or fight is not up to them—they are at the command of their king, Jesus. What matters is our relationship with him.

Prayer
Lord, keep me focused on you.

DR

The king's children

Therefore, since we have a great high priest who has gone through the heavens, Jesus the Son of God, let us hold firmly to the faith we profess. For we do not have a high priest who is unable to sympathise with our weaknesses, but we have one who has been tempted in every way, just as we are—yet was without sin. Let us then approach the throne of grace with confidence, so that we may receive mercy and find grace to help us in our time of need.

When my children were little, they sometimes used to 'visit' me while I was leading Sunday services. Usually, I'd be on the left side of the church, near the front (sitting or kneeling beside the prayer desk) and I'd become aware of a small presence beside me. I would then draw them close to me or put them on my knee until the next hymn when they would trot back to their mum. In that church it was just normal.

You are probably familiar with today's reading. Jesus, the king, is enthroned above all others, yet his throne is a throne of grace and we are encouraged to approach it confidently. Perhaps we think this means taking a deep breath, deliberately remembering our sins and shortcomings, then forcing ourselves to be calm as we plod into the king's presence. Actually, in this context, confidence comes from relationship. Just as my children pattered up to see me as if it were the most natural thing in the world, so may we patter up to the throne of grace—even if we feel that our lives are 'filthy' by God's standards. God's love for us is the driving force of his mercy and, as a good father, he knows that we are incapable of cleaning ourselves up, so longs to do it for us (Hebrews 10:22).

As Jesus is our king, we can also think of the idea of him having a court. His throne may be one of law and judgment, but it is also a throne of mercy and grace. God does not simply desire heavenly courtiers in his throne room—he wants his children there and, because of his son Jesus, we are all invited (1 John 3:1).

Prayer
Father, here I am; draw me close.

DR

Only one throne

'Those whom I love I rebuke and discipline. So be earnest, and repent. Here I am! I stand at the door and knock. If anyone hears my voice and opens the door, I will come in and eat with them, and they with me. To those who overcome, I will give the right to sit with me on my throne, just as I overcame and sat down with my Father on his throne. Those who have ears, let them hear what the Spirit says to the churches.'

Being a member of God's family is the best, most secure relationship that we can have, but it doesn't guarantee an easy life. Every family should have that right balance between acceptance and discipline, but, once we step outside the front door, who knows what blows life will deliver? When we serve Jesus the king, we inevitably oppose injustice and this can make us unpopular people (John 15:18–19). The promise in today's reading is clear, though: those who overcome the difficulties of life by inviting Jesus through their door are, in turn, invited to share his throne.

At this point, we may need to sit down and think for a bit. If our picture of heaven is of Christ the king on the throne, flanked by a host of angels and with us, part of the multitude, praising from a distance, well, that's one picture and it's easy enough to find echoes of it (in Revelation 5 and elsewhere). Here, the picture is of either a mul-tiplicity of thrones or thrones so vast that they can be occupied by a multitude. However we interpret these verses, in this picture of heaven we are all on a throne!

This is a prophetic symbol of a simple truth—that, in Christ, we are 'made perfect' (Hebrews 10:14). Not *regarded* as perfect but *made* perfect, just as he is (1 John 3:2–3). Jesus is the king, yet he is not the kind of king who rules a multitude from on high. He reigns in individual lives (the house of Jacob, the family of God). Christ the king may occupy the throne of David, but he has no intention of occupying it alone—we are all invited and included.

Prayer

Lord, thank you for inviting and including me.

DR

1 and 2 Thessalonians: letters of hope

If friends of yours came fresh to Christian faith and started to make their way as disciples of Jesus, what would you wish for them? Experienced Christian companions, perhaps, to guide them on their new journey. It would help, too, if they had time to find their feet before encountering too much nastiness, scepticism or opposition. You would certainly not want their faith to be tested by sorrow or distress while it was still taking shape.

The brand new church at Thessalonica had none of those advantages. There was persecution, some of it violent, almost from day one. The missionaries who brought the gospel had to leave town hastily, for safety's sake, and the new Christians were left to cope on their own. When some members of the church died, their fellow believers felt terribly bereft. Where had they gone when they died? What had the gospel to say about that?

The two letters to the Thessalonians were written to people who felt isolated and alone, yet they tell of hope that makes a difference, even in the worst of times. They tell, too, of deep Christian love, binding pastors and preachers to the people they have helped into faith. So perhaps there are two good reasons for reading these letters in December.

First, Advent is a season of hope. In these weeks, Christians remember that God has a sure purpose. One day this world will reflect the glory and goodness of Jesus Christ, gladly and completely. A second reason is that Christmas is often a time to reconnect with the people, relationships and memories we value most. These two letters say much about love, care and belonging, even when distance or difficulty have kept friends apart.

A bit of background might be useful here. Thessalonica is a seaport in northern Greece. It was a big, busy town in New Testament times. It was also one of the first places in Europe to hear the gospel (see Acts 17). Notice, too, the controversy and commotion the preaching caused. Some people in Thessalonica disliked the Christian message. They accused the missionaries of 'turning the world upside down… and saying that there is another king named Jesus'. They then followed them to the next town, to disrupt the preaching there, too. So Paul and his team moved on again and made contact from a distance with the Thessalonian church. These letters are part of that later stage of support and care.

John Proctor

1 THESSALONIANS 1:1–3 (NRSV)

Grace and grit

Paul, Silvanus, and Timothy, to the church of the Thessalonians in God the Father and the Lord Jesus Christ: Grace to you and peace. We always give thanks to God for all of you and mention you in our prayers, constantly remembering before our God and Father your work of faith and labour of love and steadfastness of hope in our Lord Jesus Christ.

The best mission work is often the result of teamwork. Paul was a ground-breaking apostle to the Gentiles, who longed to take the gospel to new places. Silvanus (or Silas) was a trusted companion. Like Paul, he was a man of many cultures, as at home in Jerusalem as in the towns of the Greek and Roman world. Timothy was much younger and Paul was training him for greater responsibilities, but he had important care to give in Thessalonica. Indeed, his gentler personality fitted him very well for this. The best teams usually include people of different gifts and capabilities.

Paul's letters often start with thanks. When he prayed for his friends at Thessalonica, joy flowed naturally into his writing. Indeed, this note of thanksgiving runs through half the letter (see 2:13; 3:9). Paul prayed for these people 'always... constantly' and these prayers kept his delight and gratitude lively and fresh.

The letter gives thanks for the new believers' faith, love and hope.

We meet this clutch of virtues in several places in scripture. Faith looks upwards to Jesus, love looks outwards to neighbour and the world and hope looks forwards to the future. Together they point us beyond ourselves and give orientation and stability to the Christian life. They are active qualities, attitudes to put into practice. Living them out requires effort, energy and endurance—the 'work of faith and labour of love and steadfastness of hope'.

Grace and grit go together. The love of God, the prayers of the Church and the care of friends are signs of grace. The practical demands of the gospel and the persistence needed to live it are matters of grit. Grace is given to make us gritty people, to help us live for Christ in a tough and troubled world.

Prayer

God of grace, give us courage to follow your ways in our days.

JP

Impressed by the gospel

For we know, brothers and sisters beloved by God, that he has chosen you, because our message of the gospel came to you not in word only, but also in power and in the Holy Spirit and with full conviction; just as you know what kind of persons we proved to be among you for your sake. And you became imitators of us and of the Lord, for in spite of persecution you received the word with joy inspired by the Holy Spirit, so that you became an example to all the believers in Macedonia and in Achaia.

This letter aimed to encourage, so these verses emphasise the positive—three positives, in fact. The Thessalonians had acted positively when they heard the good news. They grasped it strongly and it changed their lives. Second, Paul and his friends set a positive example to their converts. They tried to live what they taught (there is much more about this in the next chapter). The third positive is God's work. The Holy Spirit had given these new Christians a joy that must have seemed quite supernatural amid all their toils and trials. Sometimes hard-pressed people show us with special clarity the joy and grace of God. As their spirits rise above their troubles, they show that God has laid his hand on them, surely and securely.

This was what the Thessalonians had shown Paul. He was convinced that their faith was genuine, because of the difference it had made to them. 'Power... and full conviction' speak of trust and transformation that are sure marks of the Holy Spirit. God had stirred, the good news had done its work and there was no need to fear that their faith might turn out hollow. Indeed, other churches, far away, had heard the story and taken courage. If the Thessalonians had coped, they would persevere, too.

This group of new Christians had been impressed by the gospel. It was imprinted on their lives and it showed, in their faith, persistence and joy. Word gets around, when Christ's people carry burdens with courage and faith. When Christians handle pressure and come through, this in itself spreads the gospel a little more surely to new places and people.

Prayer

God of cross and resurrection, help me to reflect the life of Jesus, amid the pressures of today.

JP

1 Thessalonians 1:8–10 (NRSV)

Welcoming and waiting

For the word of the Lord has sounded forth from you not only in Macedonia and Achaia, but in every place your faith in God has become known, so that we have no need to speak about it. For the people of those regions report about us what kind of welcome we had among you, and how you turned to God from idols, to serve a living and true God, and to wait for his Son from heaven, whom he raised from the dead—Jesus, who rescues us from the wrath that is coming.

The church in Thessalonica was gaining a reputation. As Paul and his friends moved on, news of their converts travelled faster than they did. The earliest Christians were a mobile lot and, when they heard about a new church coming to life, they were quick to tell the story. Being reminded of his days in Thessalonica encouraged Paul and here he recalls how people there had welcomed the gospel. He mentions three things that are signs of the Christian life.

Christians 'turn', from whatever focus has previously claimed our lives, to putting God first. We 'serve', in our worship and life-style, the God we have trusted. We also 'wait', for the promise that this world will belong visibly and completely to Jesus Christ. It's the same trio of Christian habits we met in verse 3. Turning is a matter of faith, serving shows our love, for God and neighbour, and waiting expresses our hope, as people who trust God for the future.

Paul wanted the Thessalonians to look back thankfully and travel forwards confidently, so he reminded them of the way they had come, when they heard the gospel and committed themselves to following it. Hope is hard when times are tough. It usually helps to remember what God has already done for us.

It also helps to remember that Jesus is risen—the Church's main reason for hope is Easter. Death and evil, suffering and anger were not the last words for God's Son and they will not have the last word in God's world. When we know Jesus, we have Easter within us and ahead of us and we can go forward without fear.

Prayer

God of Easter and eternity, may hope give us energy in serving you and joy in trusting you.

JP

1 THESSALONIANS 2:5–8 (NRSV)

The way you tell them

As you know and as God is our witness, we never came with words of flattery or with a pretext for greed; nor did we seek praise from mortals, whether from you or from others, though we might have made demands as apostles of Christ. But we were gentle among you, like a nurse tenderly caring for her own children. So deeply do we care for you that we are determined to share with you not only the gospel of God but also our own selves, because you have become very dear to us.

What persuades people to start following Jesus? The gospel message carries its own power and credibility, but the way Christians live is often a big influence, too. If we share the faith with others, our life is part of the gospel they hear. The medium is the message and the messenger is part of it. Honest speech, caring deeds, trust and integrity—all contribute.

In the Greek world of New Testament times, there were plenty of travelling teachers—orators, philosophers and the like. Some were notorious for their vanity and greed. They would, it was said, do anything to please an audience, attract attention or gain honour and good contracts. Paul obviously tried hard to avoid that sort of approach and observe the very best standards of care and character. Giving, rather than gain, was what motivated him. He aimed to be gentle with people, not manipulative—to treat them with integrity and respect.

Two threads run through these verses, as they should through all our Christian service and church life. One is about proper standards in dealing with people. Christian work should always be as reputable and upright as we can possibly make it. The offence of the cross we cannot avoid, but other scandals hurt people and hinder the gospel. The second thread is about personal care. When we serve in the name of Christ, we give something of ourselves. Who we are comes out in what we do. If our attitude is generous, gentle and humble, this will show and people will see Jesus more clearly.

Reflection and prayer

Remember the people you meet—in your job, your church, your family. Ask God for wisdom to treat them honestly and honourably and with love that will show them something of Jesus.

JP

1 THESSALONIANS 2:17–3:3 (NRSV, ABRIDGED)

Absent friends

As for us, brothers and sisters, when, for a short time, we were made orphans by being separated from you—in person, not in heart—we longed with great eagerness to see you face to face… but Satan blocked our way. For what is our hope or joy or crown of boasting before our Lord Jesus at his coming? Is it not you? Yes, you are our glory and joy! Therefore when we could bear it no longer… we sent Timothy… to strengthen and encourage you for the sake of your faith, so that no one would be shaken by these persecutions.

In yesterday's reading, Paul looked back, to his weeks in Thessalonica and his care for the Christians there. In today's verses, the remembering moves forwards, to the time when he had left the town and started to be anxious about how the church would fare. It was like family ties being cut. 'In heart' he felt near to these new Christians, but 'in person' he was far away, and there was little he could do to get back. Indeed Acts (17:1–9) hints that Paul might have stirred up fresh trouble for the local Christians, if he were seen again in Thessalonica. For Paul, it felt that a malignant force had barred the way.

Timothy, however, the quiet man of the group, could travel safely. He would not attract attention, but he could support the church and keep them steady in a turbulent situation. So Paul sent him and waited —impatiently, one imagines—for him to report back.

This church really mattered to Paul. As he looked forward to the 'appearing of the Lord Jesus', he wanted his converts there to rejoice with him. He had involved himself in their care, prayed for them and urged them on. Now he longed for the final fruition of the growth and grace he had seen in them. He wanted them to press on with Christ and share heaven's glory.

In this season of Advent hope, we too may look forward. One day, the whole Church, from across the world and the generations, will gather with Jesus. We shall be separate and strangers no longer.

Prayer

Pray for Christians in another land, whom you know something about, but whom you may never meet, until Christ comes.

JP

Wishing well

Now may our God and Father himself and our Lord Jesus direct our way to you. And may the Lord make you increase and abound in love for one another and for all, just as we abound in love for you. And may he so strengthen your hearts in holiness that you may be blameless before our God and Father at the coming of our Lord Jesus with all his saints.

'If you had three wishes…' It's the stuff of children's stories, to imagine we could ask for anything, but it's also part of Christian prayer, to let God know the desires of our heart. We ought to share with God the things that matter deeply to us and expect God to get involved. There is plenty in scripture to encourage this attitude and prompt us to pray with confidence (for example, Mark 11:22–25).

These two Thessalonian letters include a handful of little 'wish prayers'. Today's reading is one, and others come at 1 Thessalonians 5:23 and 2 Thessalonians 2:16; 3:5 and 16. The wording means 'I wish that God would …' and this first prayer contains three wishes. One wish is that God will find a way for Paul to return to Thessalonica. Timothy has reported that the Christians there are doing well (1 Thessalonians 3:6), but Paul still longs to reconnect with them himself. The second wish concerns relationships within the church, that they will become a more loving fellowship. The third is that they will live holy lives and be prepared to meet Christ in glory.

Paul will have more to say about some of these concerns and desires. Indeed, this little prayer is a hinge in the middle of the letter, as the focus moves from remembering and thanksgiving in chapters 1—3, to pastoral guidance and advice in chapters 4—5. Paul has concerns to share with his readers, direction to offer them, challenges to put and assurances to give. When he prays here about their relationships and their readiness for Christ's coming, he is preparing for advice to be given. There are delicate matters to discuss and even the best advice may be of little use if it is not accompanied by careful and persistent prayer.

Reflection

'What a privilege to carry everything to God in prayer.'

Joseph Scriven,
'What a friend we have in Jesus'

JP

1 THESSALONIANS 4:1, 3–4, 11–12 (NRSV, ABRIDGED)

Keep yourself

Finally, brothers and sisters, we ask and urge you in the Lord Jesus that, as you learned from us how you ought to live and to please God... you should do so more and more... For this is the will of God, your sanctification: that you abstain from fornication; that each one of you know how to control your own body in holiness and honour... aspire to live quietly, to mind your own affairs, and to work with your hands, as we directed you, so that you may behave properly towards outsiders and be dependent on no one.

We cannot know all that Timothy told Paul after visiting Thessalonica. Certainly the Christians were persisting in their faith (3:6–8), but after a new commitment of this kind, there would have been habits and customs to unlearn and fresh ways to adopt. New friendships would take time to form, as Christians got used to belonging together in Christ. The two issues Paul tackles in today's reading may have been part of this process.

Christian teaching on sex and marriage was out of kilter with a lot that went on in the Greek and Roman world. Married men, especially, were sometimes very casual about their loyalties, but Paul reckoned that faithfulness and self-control in sex and marriage were important issues. They were marks of holiness, signs that a person's life belonged to God, as well as a way of showing respect to promises and partners.

The final verses about quiet and self-sufficient living suggest that some church members had become too dependent on others. Of course, some people—the young and old, for example—have to depend on others, but they are not Paul's concern here. He worked hard when he visited Thessalonica (2:9) and he wants the Christians there to do the same, if they can. These verses are about Christian love, and love often involves giving when I can and taking only when I must.

Keep yourself under control, keep yourself to yourself and keep yourself by your own labour. While this advice certainly does not cover the whole of Christian conduct, it may be important for many of us, much of the time, as we live out our new life in Christ.

Prayer

God of wisdom and goodness, may my life express your holiness and reflect your love for my neighbour.

JP

1 THESSALONIANS 4:13–14, 16–17 (NRSV, ABRIDGED)

Together with the Lord

But we do not want you to be uninformed, brothers and sisters, about those who have died, so that you may not grieve as others do who have no hope. For since we believe that Jesus died and rose again, even so, through Jesus, God will bring with him those who have died... For the Lord himself... will descend from heaven, and the dead in Christ will rise first. Then we who are alive, who are left, will be caught up in the clouds together with them to meet the Lord in the air; and so we will be with the Lord for ever.

Christians grieve, too. When death breaks in, we weep and hurt—but friends in Christ are not lost. We will meet again and be with the Lord for ever.

Advent is a time in the Christian year when many churches speak about the second coming of Jesus Christ. This coming is the focus of today's reading. It all starts, like so much in our faith, at Easter. Because 'Jesus died and rose again', he will share his risen life with his people. His resurrection guarantees ours.

Paul's language—'caught up to meet the Lord'—may refer to a custom in the ancient world, when a major public figure came to town. A company of people would have travelled with the dignitary and then a group of citizens would have gone out along the road to escort him (it was usually 'him') back to their city. If we think of Jesus' coming like this, Paul may have meant that the 'dead in Christ', who are presently near to Jesus, will rise to join him on his journey from heaven to earth as his travelling companions. Then those of us who are alive, waiting in hope and faith, will be gathered up to meet him, too, so all will be together, as he comes to judge and renew the world.

Whether or not this is exactly what Paul meant, these verses were never intended as mere speculation about a remote future. They were given as pastoral care for a church in shock, comfort for a people experiencing sadness and courage for friends under stress. When Christians grieve, as we must, we grieve in hope.

Prayer

Lord of hope, keep me steady, that I may share with others the strength of Christ.

JP

1 THESSALONIANS 5:1–4, 8 (NRSV, ABRIDGED)

Blind date?

Now concerning the times and the seasons, brothers and sisters... you yourselves know very well that the day of the Lord will come like a thief in the night. When they say, 'There is peace and security', then sudden destruction will come upon them, as labour pains come upon a pregnant woman, and there will be no escape! But you, beloved, are not in darkness, for that day to surprise you like a thief... But since we belong to the day, let us be sober, and put on the breastplate of faith and love, and for a helmet the hope of salvation.

There are two alternatives to hope, but neither is much help to us. If we have no hope, we run out of optimism and our mental and spiritual batteries get very low. If we have too much hope of the wrong kind, we may waste our enthusiasm chasing shadows. If we always want to know the precise timing of God's plans, we may be consumed by frustration and disappointment.

Yesterday's reading was about what Christ's coming will bring, which we can know. Today's verses are about when it will be, which we don't know. Although we cannot predict when that will be, we can prepare. Here are four images of the event.

The thief: The image of Jesus as a burglar, arriving stealthily, comes from the Lord himself (Matthew 24:43, for example). A thief never gives notice; you need to stay awake.

Pregnancy and labour: When a woman's time is near, she wants to be ready—bag packed, help at hand, and so on—but events can unfold very suddenly.

Night and day: Dawn comes abruptly on 'the day of the Lord'. The light will be difficult to get used to. We need to start living in the light of the gospel now.

The armour of God: Faith, hope and love (those three again!) provide spiritual protection and help us to be ready for whatever changes or surprises time and eternity may bring.

I wonder if this letter helped the Thessalonians to look forward to Christ's coming, without worrying when it might be. It has certainly helped many people since to apply themselves to Christian basics and stop chasing the shadows of details, dates and diaries.

Prayer
God of the ages, help me to live for the future by trusting you for today.

JP

Leading questions

But we appeal to you, brothers and sisters, to respect those who labour among you, and have charge of you in the Lord and admonish you; esteem them very highly in love because of their work. Be at peace among yourselves. And we urge you, beloved, to admonish the idlers, encourage the faint-hearted, help the weak, be patient with all of them.

Finding leaders in a brand new community of Christian converts must have been a tricky business, but Paul tried to do this wherever he went. Then, after he left, responsible people would make an effort to look after their fellow Christians. When he wrote to churches, he sometimes covered leadership issues, to help the elders, bishops or deacons to do their jobs properly.

We do not know who led the church in Thessalonica. Jason appears as a leading figure in Acts 17, but he is not named in these two letters. Whoever the leaders were, Timothy must have reported positively on them, for Paul makes no criticism of their attitudes or actions. He evidently reckoned these were the right people for the job and he wanted to encourage and affirm them in their work. So what does a church owe to its leaders? What do leaders owe their church?

Care for individuals is a vital part of leadership. People are all different and the last verse above urges the Thessalonian leaders to remember that. There were 'idlers' to stir, 'faint-hearted' people to sustain and 'weak' brothers and sisters to strengthen. The only thing we all have in common is that our leaders need to be patient with us. None of us is as wise, gracious or cooperative as we might like to think. Most of us will be grateful for Christian leaders who have taken time with us, coped with our oddities and helped us to grow in Christ.

A church owes its leaders respect, honour and love—and all the members owe one another their best efforts at peace and maintaining harmony and care. A church determined to quarrel is impossible to lead anywhere, let alone towards spiritual maturity and effective Christian witness.

Reflection and prayer

Pray for the Christian leaders you know. Ask God to give them the patience they need. Pray for the church or fellowship to which you belong. Ask God to give it peace.

JP

1 Thessalonians 5:15–22 (NRSV)

Last orders

> See that none of you repays evil for evil, but always seek to do good to one another and to all. Rejoice always, pray without ceasing, give thanks in all circumstances; for this is the will of God in Christ Jesus for you. Do not quench the Spirit. Do not despise the words of prophets, but test everything; hold fast to what is good; abstain from every form of evil.

These snippets of teaching seem almost an afterthought, as Paul's writing runs towards a close, but he surely had reason for including them. This letter was written to Christians under pressure, who had faced persecution for their faith. After writing about hope and the far horizon, Paul wanted to say something more immediate, to leave his readers with words to which they could respond. So here is some practical spirituality, an outlook that seeks God's best in every situation.

Peace is the first concern: revenge is out. When other people curse us, Christians bless them in return. We pray for them and, if they need help, we do not refuse. Prayer is the second theme. This must be the lifeblood of our days, pulsing through every experience, carrying energy and strength to each part of our living. We may not want to give thanks for every circumstance, but we may still praise God, whatever happens around us. Prophecy is the third topic.

Christians should expect God to comfort and challenge them through the insight of others. Sometimes another person's word is like a gift from God, a shaft of light into the fog of our lives. Not every plausible bit of advice is a word from the Lord, however. We have the right and duty to work out our own response.

All this sounds a little like teaching Jesus gave in the Sermon on the Mount. See Matthew 5:38–44 for the first slice, verses 11–12 for the second and 7:15–23 for the third. Quite a number of Jesus' sayings surface in the New Testament letters and these were surely handed down among the earliest Christians. Of course, for them as for us, remembering the teaching is only a first step. We need to put it into practice.

Prayer

Lord Jesus Christ, help me to live by your word, in my faith, my prayer and my actions.

JP

2 THESSALONIANS 1:3–5 (NRSV)

Grace and growth

We must always give thanks to God for you, brothers and sisters, as is right, because your faith is growing abundantly, and the love of every one of you for one another is increasing. Therefore we ourselves boast of you among the churches of God for your steadfastness and faith during all your persecutions and the afflictions that you are enduring. This is evidence of the righteous judgment of God, and is intended to make you worthy of the kingdom of God, for which you are also suffering.

The second Thessalonian letter is much shorter than the first and returns often to themes and concerns from the earlier letter. Some of its material is fresh, for there have been changes and confusions at Thessalonica and the church needs new advice about these, but much of the letter contains teaching we have heard before. Time has moved on, but many of the church's needs remain and Paul wants to repeat guidance that he has already given.

The letter starts with a thanksgiving prayer. Paul thanks God for the way the Thessalonians have advanced in their faith, their growth in love and courage under persecution. The opposition facing the church has persisted, but Paul can see purpose in it. It shows that these Christians are genuine—something real has happened in their lives and God's strength is sustaining them. In time, such hardships will produce a solid Christian maturity, preparing the believers for God's coming kingdom.

When we are going through the mangle ourselves, it never seems at all spiritual. Paul's words suggest, though, that even our worst experiences can do something for others, by showing them Christ in us, and can do something for us, by bringing us nearer to Christ. The Thessalonian church must have weathered the storm for this letter survived. Indeed, it seems that pressure brought them closer together, for Paul says their 'love is increasing'. That is surely an example and challenge to us, to love one another more strongly when times are tough. To do so is a sign that the grace of God is at work among us.

Prayer

Pray for someone you know who is in the midst of trouble or suffering. Then think what you could do to show them God's love.

JP

Waiting time

As to the coming of our Lord Jesus Christ and our being gathered together to him, we beg you, brothers and sisters, not to be quickly shaken in mind or alarmed, either by spirit or by word or by letter, as though from us, to the effect that the day of the Lord is already here. Let no one deceive you in any way; for that day will not come unless the rebellion comes first and the lawless one is revealed, the one destined for destruction. He opposes and exalts himself above every so-called god or object of worship, so that he takes his seat in the temple of God, declaring himself to be God.

Some of the Thessalonians thought that the day of the Lord had already arrived. Perhaps Paul did not know where they got this strange idea, but he certainly wanted to talk them out of it. If they thought they had missed out on Christ's coming, they would panic. In this situation his earlier teaching on the suddenness of the day (1 Thessalonians 5:1–11) would not help much. Paul's readers needed to know that there is an order in the unfolding of God's purposes, so these verses talk about 'the lawless one'.

Some other New Testament passages speak of an 'Antichrist', as if the whole of humanity's opposition to God can somehow cluster around a particular figure in history. Paul, it seems, expected an increase in evil in the world before Christ comes to judge and save.

Attempts to name this evil and identify it with a single person may be too simple. Antichrist figures surface throughout history. There were assaults on the Jerusalem Temple by the Syrian king Antiochus, a couple of centuries before Jesus, and by the Emperor Caligula in AD40. There was lawlessness in the persecution Paul faced in Thessalonica and elsewhere. In our own memories, Hitler, Stalin and Pol Pot appalled decent people around the world, yet every one of them has faded or fallen. Paul looked for something bigger, nastier, more dreadful and more final.

This seems an awful vision, but it is good to know that even time's ugliest evil is temporary. The reign of Christ will endure for ever; we need not panic.

Prayer

God of truth and power, when I see evil in the world, help me to face it with faith and without fear.

JP

Bonded in God

Finally, brothers and sisters, pray for us, so that the word of the Lord may spread rapidly and be glorified everywhere, just as it is among you, and that we may be rescued from wicked and evil people; for not all have faith. But the Lord is faithful; he will strengthen you and guard you from the evil one. And we have confidence in the Lord concerning you, that you are doing and will go on doing the things that we command. May the Lord direct your hearts to the love of God and to the steadfastness of Christ.

As this short letter moves towards a close, Paul reflects on the challenges ahead, for him and his companions and for the Christians in Thessalonica. He has a gospel to carry, fresh fields to sow with the word and a world to win. They have pressures to bear, commands to follow and a new pattern of life to sustain. If we put it this way, their situations seem very different.

Paul, though, saw common threads in the two sets of experiences. Mission was one. He wanted God's word to spread, 'just as it is among you'. Having planted the gospel in Thessalonica, a regional centre and a major port, Paul realised that the church there could make its own missionary impact. People would be convinced by the Christians' faith, hope and love. The message would get around.

Suffering was another shared experience. Paul asked to be 'rescued from wicked people', kept clear of their hands and schemes. In the same way, the church in Thessalonica needed the protection of God as they put up with the opposition of neighbours. This gospel was controversial and costly to follow.

Prayer would be a constant need. Christians can support each other by taking time with God and naming concerns and friends before God. 'Pray for us', says the letter. Then, at the end of the passage, there is another little wish prayer: 'we pray for you, we want God to help you'. These prayers are straightforward but profound. They ask for effective work, protection, love and endurance. We could pray these blessings for many a Christian, almost anywhere in God's world.

Reflection and prayer

Give thanks for people who have prayed for you across the years and for anyone who prays for you today.

JP

Good news of great joy

Luke was the doctor who travelled with the apostle Paul. Two of the New Testament books, Acts and the Gospel of Luke, were written by him. There is an energy and excitement and an underlying sense of curiosity about his style that appeals to me as a writer and a reader. Luke really does want to communicate his discoveries to us and he clearly feels that a little extra detail is always helpful. He is the only Gospel writer to record an event in the life of Jesus at the age of 12 and his account of the period before Jesus' birth in Bethlehem is filled with fresh material that he must have personally researched. Every now and then, as we shall see, a particular phrase or way of expressing an idea suggests that a little nugget of personal experience has been woven into the text and the story is all the richer for it.

If I have to write about the Christmas story I would rather respond to Luke's account than to that in any of the other Gospels, but I have to be honest and say that a pall of weariness descends on me whenever I am asked to do something about events surrounding the birth of Christ. I think this may be because I have had to listen to more talks and sermons about the 'real meaning of Christmas' than any sane person should have to endure. If I hear one more person sternly reminding me that I mustn't get caught up in the commercialism of it all I think I shall go raving mad and rush out to spend huge amounts of money that I haven't got on things that no one really wants.

Am I saying that the Christmas story means nothing to me? No, I am not, but I am saying that those events in Bethlehem 2000 years ago were so ordinary and so extraordinary all at the same time that I can no longer see them in the context of a simple equation about commercialism and austerity.

Jesus was born, that is the point. It goes on being the point and the pattern in the middle of wars and sickness and horror and disappointment and death and ordinariness and the fear of oblivion. Whatever the scenario, Jesus, amazingly, can and will be born into it and, because of that, thank God, there will always be hope.

Adrian Plass

Joining up the dots

Many have undertaken to draw up an account of the things that have been fulfilled among us, just as they were handed down to us by those who from the first were eye witnesses and servants of the word. With this in mind, since I myself have carefully investigated everything from the beginning, I too decided to write an orderly account for you, most excellent Theophilus, so that you may know the certainty of the things you have been taught.

As far as we can tell, Luke was a Gentile and a man of considerable learning. Perhaps because of this, his accounts in this Gospel and in Acts combine objectivity and involvement as well as being very well written. A sort of cross between Alan Whicker and Louis Theroux? Who knows? Isn't it fascinating, though? I love the idea that Luke, anxious to join up all the dots for his friend Theophilus—certainly a Roman and probably a Christian—has travelled far and wide to discover what actually happened during the life of Jesus and speak to some of the people who knew him.

What a television documentary that would make! Can you imagine, for instance, Luke speaking with nervous excitement to the camera as he draws nearer and nearer to the place where the mother of Jesus, Mary herself, is living? The climax would be electrifying. Suddenly, there she is, probably quite elderly by now, head bowed and humble, but more than ready to talk about the succession of extraordinary experiences that puzzled her and pierced her heart and ultimately filled her with a depth of joy that she could never have anticipated.

Of course, Luke had no recording equipment or cameras to assist him in storing the information he gathered, but he probably didn't need them. Perhaps he jotted down the old lady's stories in some form or other, but her words must have burned themselves into his memory. This was Mary, the one chosen by God to bring his Son into this world. What a privilege!

How would he have begun the interview? I have no idea, but I can guess: 'Mary, tell me about the beginning. Tell me how it all started.'

Prayer

Thank you, Father, for Luke and his painstaking storytelling. Help us to reach a new depth of understanding through his account.

AP

The inevitable pattern

In the sixth month of Elizabeth's pregnancy, God sent the angel Gabriel to Nazareth, a town in Galilee, to a virgin pledged to be married to a man named Joseph, a descendant of David. The virgin's name was Mary. The angel went to her and said, 'Greetings, you who are highly favoured! The Lord is with you.' Mary was greatly troubled at his words and wondered what kind of greeting this might be. But the angel said to her, 'Do not be afraid, Mary, you have found favour with God.'

A touch of irony here. Over the last 50 years or so, we have endured a veritable avalanche of so-called Christian books, most of which advocate and even prescribe an attitude of joyful acceptance to everything God throws at us. It all sounds so worthy and wonderful, but takes no account of the fact that life, Christian or otherwise, is simply not like that. Sometimes events knock us flat and it takes a while to get back on to our feet and learn to trust in the ultimate power and care with which God looks after and keeps safe the most important part of us. This brief account of Mary's first encounter with an angel offers a very early template for how to proceed with the business of honestly owning the truth about ourselves. Bear in mind that the information about her response on this occasion can only have come from Mary herself.

'So,' says Luke, 'an angel appears and says that you are greatly blessed. What a thing to happen! You must have felt wonderful.'

'Wonderful?' replies Mary. 'I didn't feel wonderful at all. I was confused and worried. I had no idea what it all meant.'

Exactly—and that pattern must have continued throughout the next 33 years of Mary's life. Greatly blessed and deeply troubled. Raised, lowered and tossed about like a small boat in a huge ocean. That, if we are honest, is the pattern in most of our lives as well. Those who have the capacity for obedience to the strange will of God will undoubtedly be highly favoured, but they will also know times of fear and bewilderment. Mary would understand.

Prayer

Father, thank you for Mary's straightforwardness and honesty. Help us not to talk nonsense about our faith.

AP

A trip to the fairground

'You will conceive and give birth to a son, and you are to call him Jesus. He will be great and will be called the Son of the Most High. The Lord God will give him the throne of his father David, and he will reign over the house of Jacob for ever; his kingdom will never end.' 'How will this be,' Mary asked the angel, 'since I am a virgin?' The angel answered, 'The Holy Spirit will come on you, and the power of the Most High will overshadow you. So the holy one to be born will be called the Son of God. Even Elizabeth your relative is going to have a child in her old age, and she who was said to be unable to conceive is in her sixth month. For no word from God will ever fail.' 'I am the Lord's servant,' Mary answered. 'May it be to me according to your word.' Then the angel left her.

The 'rollercoaster' metaphor is vastly overused but does adequately describe what is happening to Mary here. If she was troubled before, the news that mystical conception would result in the pregnancy and birth of the Son of the Most High must have equalled the sensation of plunging instantly down a vertical precipice. Her reply to the angel is a remarkable distillation of all that confusion and she asks a very sensible question. 'How can I have a baby if I'm a virgin?' It is a small point, but important.

Back to the frantic fairground ride. The Holy Spirit will come on her. Weird, but leave it for now. The power of the Most High will overshadow her. Er, carry on then. The one to be born will be called the Son of God. Right, got it. Her cousin Elizabeth is already in the sixth month of her pregnancy. What?!

I may be wrong, but I have always fancied this last bit of news might have swung it for Mary as far as acceptance was concerned. Something real and checkable and lodged in a real belly. Elizabeth? A baby? At *her* age? Anything's possible! God is on the move. You don't argue. You just go with him. 'I'm in', says Mary.

Reflection

If you get caught up in the excitement of God's plans, you don't always have to understand what's going on.

AP

Dancing round the room

At that time Mary got ready and hurried to a town in the hill country of Judea, where she entered Zechariah's home and greeted Elizabeth. When Elizabeth heard Mary's greeting, the baby leaped in her womb, and Elizabeth was filled with the Holy Spirit. In a loud voice she exclaimed: 'Blessed are you among women, and blessed is the child you will bear! But why am I so favoured, that the mother of my Lord should come to me? As soon as the sound of your greeting reached my ears, the baby in my womb leaped for joy. Blessed is she who has believed that the Lord would fulfil his promises to her!'

We can't blame her for checking it out, can we? After all, if the bit about Elizabeth being six months gone was accurate, then the rest, obscure as it may have seemed, was probably true as well. 'Mary got ready and hurried.' I love that little group of words—such a charmingly small but significant memory. Surely it can only have come from the mother of Jesus herself. She flung things around, shoved a few clothes in a bag and rushed off to see the miracle pregnancy for herself. Any fatigue from the journey must have been dispelled by the eruptive nature of her encounter with the older woman. Not only was Elizabeth well and truly pregnant, but she loudly confirmed the message of the angel and passed on the electrifying news that her baby had actually jumped around with joy in her womb on realising that the reason for his very existence was only a couple of feet away. Did people hold hands and dance round the room in those days? If they didn't, I bet Elizabeth and Mary wanted to.

As I read Luke's endearing account, I am struck once more by a zinging tension between the seamless interaction of spiritual and secular in the Bible and the po-faced, inaccessible way in which scriptural stories have so often been presented to the world. It is in real life, among real people that the Holy Spirit engages with the real world. Don't look for God in the dank, echoing caverns of religious pomposity. He isn't there. He is far more likely to be found dancing on a hillside with some very ordinary people.

Reflection
Remember, Emmanuel—
God with us.

AP

The long haul

In those days Caesar Augustus issued a decree that a census should be taken of the entire Roman world. (This was the first census that took place while Quirinius was governor of Syria.) And everyone went to their own town to register. So Joseph also went up from the town of Nazareth in Galilee to Judea, to Bethlehem the town of David, because he belonged to the house and line of David. He went there to register with Mary, who was pledged to be married to him and was expecting a child. While they were there, the time came for the baby to be born, and she gave birth to her first-born, a son. She wrapped him in cloths and placed him in a manger, because there was no guest room available for them.

Nazareth is 80 miles from Bethlehem. A doddle by car nowadays. A train would be fine, too. Bus? Slow and long, but just bearable. Donkey? Eighty miles along rough tracks, bouncing on the bony back of a clip-clopping, frequently stopping, probably very stubborn old mule when you're nine months' pregnant—that is a big ask.

Isn't that the point, though? The fact that we are on our way to do something that is (we hope) useful for God is no guarantee that the road, actual or metaphorical, will be smoothed for us. Mary was on her way to a place where the image of the invisible God, the saviour of the world, was to be born. Surely something more comfortable could have been sorted out for her? A BMW? A Holiday Inn? No, it was nothing like that. Generally speaking, it won't be for us either.

Bridget and I recently flew to Australia for a speaking tour. Halfway through that eternal flight I felt as if I could have abandoned my faith and sold my children into slavery in exchange for four hours just being horizontal. That deal was unavailable with Qantas, so my faith and my children are more or less safe. It's the same process, though. Physically, emotionally or spiritually, we have to accept the problems of the journey if we want to get to the place where the brilliant things happen. Sometimes that journey is very hard indeed. The cross is another good example of how hard it is even for Jesus.

Prayer

Wake us to the realities of following you, Lord. Some of us are a bit spoilt.

AP

The pattern

And there were shepherds living out in the fields near by, keeping watch over their flocks at night. An angel of the Lord appeared to them, and the glory of the Lord shone around them, and they were terrified. But the angel said to them, 'Do not be afraid. I bring you good news of great joy that will be for all the people. Today in the town of David a Saviour has been born to you; he is the Messiah, the Lord. This will be a sign to you: you will find a baby wrapped in cloths and lying in a manger.' Suddenly a great company of the heavenly host appeared with the angel, praising God and saying, 'Glory to God in the highest heaven, and on earth peace to those on whom his favour rests.'

Heaven could be a shock for some. A bit of a cliché, but in the context of this passage it bears repeating. Christians pay lip-service to Jesus' teaching that the first will be last and vice versa, but do many people really believe that? Can it possibly be true that the smart, worldly, famous ones who invest mainly in themselves will have to give way to 'little' folk who have no standing in the world, but quietly give themselves and all they have to the sick, naked and imprisoned because they love Jesus and want to serve him?

What about the fabulously rich? I know wealthy people who are wonderfully generous and open to the leading of the Holy Spirit, but I know others who are not. I suspect that in their heart of hearts is an ingrained belief that, when push comes to shove, even at the gates of heaven, the power of money will see them through. Jesus told us to store up treasures in heaven (Matthew 6:20). He wasn't joking and it's more than a metaphor. Heavenly treasure is not Monopoly money and it won't disappear into the coffers of some failing bank. It will be waiting there, to be spent by those who have earned it. Any other currency will be utterly worthless.

Usually the shepherds would be the last to hear about anything. When the most important event in the history of the world happened in Bethlehem, they were the first. It's a pattern.

Reflection

Eternity is a very long time. Invest.

AP

Do the next thing

> When the angels had left them and gone into heaven, the shepherds said to one another, 'Let's go to Bethlehem and see this thing that has happened, which the Lord has told us about.' So they hurried off and found Mary and Joseph, and the baby, who was lying in the manger. When they had seen him, they spread the word concerning what had been told them about this child, and all who heard it were amazed at what the shepherds said to them. But Mary treasured up all these things and pondered them in her heart. The shepherds returned, glorifying and praising God for all the things they had heard and seen, which were just as they had been told.

t wasn't a con. They hadn't been tricked. Probably for the first time in their lives, those smelly shepherds were the ones with the hot news and the personal experience. Everything the angels predicted had come true. What a joy, what a blast to be able to go from the place where that manger stood and amaze the locals with their account of angels, a stable and the baby who was—guess what—the Messiah! Two things made this happiness possible for them.

First, they did what they were told. So many worthwhile experiences begin with simple acts of affirmation or obedience. Do the next thing—not a bad motto for followers of Jesus. If God shows you something, follow it up. That's what the shepherds did and they were rewarded.

Second, they don't seem to have embroidered the experience of being led to the place where that little Son of God was lying. They were still smelly shepherds, but now they were smelly shepherds who had received a favour from God. That's all Christians have ever been—smelly, sinful men and women unexpectedly favoured by God. We can rave about the author of our faith all we want, but, as soon as we rave about ourselves, everything goes terribly pear-shaped.

As for Mary, well, she tucked the shepherds' visit away in the storehouse of her memory, like a little nugget of gold, and waited to see what would happen next. What else could she do?

Prayer

Lord, sometimes we forget that we have treasure from the past stored away in our memories. Thank you for your gifts to us.

AP

The most important thing

On the eighth day, when it was time to circumcise the child, he was named Jesus, the name the angel had given him before he was conceived... Now there was a man in Jerusalem called Simeon, who was righteous and devout. He was waiting for the consolation of Israel, and the Holy Spirit was on him. It had been revealed to him by the Holy Spirit that he would not die before he had seen the Lord's Messiah. Moved by the Spirit, he went into the temple courts.

Another anecdote directly from Mary? A further instance of God bringing different strands together in order to add yet more to his tapestry of majesty and mystery. For Mary it was clearly mostly mystery. Mystery after mystery, in fact, surrounding and enfolding an ordinary little baby who probably chuckled and goo-gooed and expelled unpleasant substances at inappropriate times like any other baby. Almost all mothers are intensely proud of their offspring, even when they are not saviours of the world. I wonder if Mary held her son with a little extra care every time one of these extraordinary events occurred.

It reminds me of *The Antiques Roadshow*, a popular TV programme in which people bring along their possessions to be assessed and valued by experts. Occasionally, an old china pot that has been filled with junk and left in a garden shed for years will turn out to be worth thousands of pounds. The amazed owner looks at his or her unsuspected treasure with a new respect, often reflecting with horror on the casual way it had been tossed into the back of the car before setting out that morning. From now on they will handle it with enormous care and give it the prominence in their home that its value merits.

At the risk of sounding like a bad sermon, I would suggest that a few of us Christians have dumped our treasure in some undistinguished corner, having forgotten or perhaps never really understood its true value. It is our responsibility to carry Jesus humbly and proudly through the world, allowing the mystery and the majesty to attend his presence. We must be careful, though. We mustn't drop him. He is the most important thing we will ever hold.

Prayer

Father, teach us to value your precious, precious Son.

AP

Salvation is in his arms

When the parents brought in the child Jesus to do for him what the custom of the Law required, Simeon took him in his arms and praised God, saying: 'Sovereign Lord, as you have promised, you may now dismiss your servant in peace. For my eyes have seen your salvation, which you have prepared in the sight of all nations: a light for revelation to the Gentiles, and the glory of your people Israel.'

Here is a man who is able to appreciate a Christmas present. What a moment for Simeon! At last, probably after waiting for years and years, God kept his promise and allowed the old man to hold the salvation of humanity in his arms before departing peacefully from the world. I wonder why God granted this favour. Simeon was righteous and devout. Perhaps that was it. 'You're a good chap, Simeon. Is there something you'd really like?'

'Well, now you mention it, I would *love* to see the Messiah just once before I die.'

'No problem.'

I raise the question of why God gave his servant such a gift because, to be honest, I'm a bit jealous. The story of Simeon would normally be used in Bible notes and sermons to show that we should be patient because God will keep his promises in the end. The problem is that most of us don't have the kind of clear and specific promises from God that

Simeon had. We ask for help with important things, hope that God will answer our prayers and do our best to trust that scriptural promises will be fulfilled, but there's not a lot of the 'I'll meet you by the back entrance to the railway station at 7.25' experiences that you read about in some of the testimony books. I have no clever answers to this, but a couple of things spring to mind.

One is that, as mentioned, Simeon was righteous and devout. Personally, I don't wish to explore that any further here, but I will later. You can reflect on it more, if you like. The second is that I probably tend not to ask God for narrowly specific things. Once I've had a look at point one I might just try that.

Prayer

*Father, if it's all right with you,
I really would like…*

AP

Heavy-duty truth

The child's father and mother marvelled at what was said about him. Then Simeon blessed them and said to Mary, his mother: 'This child is destined to cause the falling and rising of many in Israel, and to be a sign that will be spoken against, so that the thoughts of many hearts will be revealed. And a sword will pierce your own soul too.'

This is a heavy-duty pronouncement, each section landing like a blow from a mallet. Have you ever been prophesied over or given words from God? I have and the experiences vary enormously. Many of these communications have had a fluffy feel about them: God loves me and would have me do this or that vague thing on his behalf or God is preparing a mighty work and, through love and prayer, his purposes will produce fruit in abundance. There's nothing really wrong with that sort of stuff, of course. They are fine sentiments and one might be tempted to say that, in a sense, it doesn't really matter if they are genuine words from God or not. They can't do much harm and they might even do some good. It does matter, though, because the real thing is almost certainly going to be far less vague and much more genuinely utilitarian. Here is a good example of that.

Simeon's words, delivered uncompromisingly to a couple who are possibly starting to think that, mysteriously, their marvellous child might bring nothing but good for tune, are a preparation and a warning. Little baby Jesus, so safe in his mother's arms as the prophe speaks, will one day be responsible for the rise and fall of many in Israel. People will speak out against everything that he represents thereby revealing their true hearts. Mary's heart will be all but broken by the pain of witnessing the apparent self-destruction of her son.

Not a very cheery list, but perhaps Mary was already beginning to understand that, when 'Aslan is on the move' (as C.S. Lewis would say) and has something to say, even the bad news from him is the only news worth hearing, simply because it is the truth.

Prayer

Father, there are times when we trivialise your gifts and dilute their effectiveness. We pray for boldness, discretion and wisdom so that, when we speak for you, we speak nothing but the truth.

AP

At that very moment

There was also a prophet, Anna, the daughter of Phanuel, of the tribe of Asher. She was very old; she had lived with her husband seven years after her marriage, and then had been a widow for eighty-four years. She never left the temple but worshipped night and day, fasting and praying. Coming up to them at that very moment, she gave thanks to God and spoke about the child to all who were looking forward to the redemption of Jerusalem.

'At that very moment'—those four words jumped out at me from this passage. Why? They have the ring of conversational authenticity about them.

'It was amazing, Doctor Luke! Simeon had just finished speaking to me and a lady called Anna came up to us *at that very moment* and thanked God for our baby. She was telling everyone that he would be the one to redeem Jerusalem. He stared at her with his big round eyes for a moment and then he burped!'

All right, I guessed the burp, but it must have been something like that.

I have a very soft spot for Anna, brief though her appearance is in the New Testament. According to my maths, she must have been alive for more than a century. Assuming she got married at 17, she would have been 24 when her husband died and 24 plus 84 comes to 108. Imagine that, 84 years without a husband, 84 years

in the temple, 84 years of worship, prayer, fasting and waiting for God to do whatever he wanted in her life. Now, quite unexpectedly, she is offered the cameo part of a lifetime. Those 84 years of consistent preparation allow her to play the part perfectly.

I get quite a lot of letters from very elderly ladies who have led active lives in the past and they frequently include a comment about being old and retired and widowed and not very useful any more. Well, think again, ladies. Think about Anna. Think about the fact that God may have some crucial role for you to play, whatever your age. Just picture it. You will be feeling particularly useless one day and suddenly it will happen—at that very moment.

Reflection

There are no useless or redundant people in the kingdom of God, regardless of age or circumstance.

AP

Luke 2:39–40 (TNIV)

The right thing

When Joseph and Mary had done everything required by the Law of the Lord, they returned to Galilee to their own town of Nazareth. And the child grew and became strong; he was filled with wisdom, and the grace of God was on him.

I was reading the autobiography of a friend the other day and one bit of it annoyed me. Most of the book was a fairly detailed account of how God had worked in his life as he moved from early childhood on to schooling, then through university and, finally, into the area of ministry that he has successfully pursued for the last 25 years or so. There were lots of highs and lows and spiritual thrills and spills plus analysis of the movement and effect of the Holy Spirit in his life. It was a good read and I was fully absorbed, until I came to a bit where he simply said, 'For the next ten years, my wife and I lived in a village just outside Northampton.'

What was this? Ten years doing what? Ten years feeling, praying, discovering, learning, understanding what exactly in a village just outside Northampton? How could my friend have decided that a whole decade of his life was so lacking in interest that not a single day was worth recalling?

'It's stupid,' I said to myself, 'just plain stupid to leave people wondering why a whole ten years isn't worth mentioning in a book that's supposed to be an honest account of the writer's life.'

Things do irritate me sometimes. I was fuming. I rang him up.

'Great book,' I said, so that he would go on listening, 'but what about the ten years with your wife in the village near Northampton? Why aren't we allowed to know about that?'

Silence.

'Well, we were happy, and it was all about us, and it was—you know—the right thing.'

Ah. Happy. All about us. The right thing.

Suddenly I understood completely. I also understand now why we know almost nothing about the early life of Jesus with his mother and father. It was happy. It was about them. It was the right thing.

Prayer

Father, thank you so much for those times when it is right simply to be us and enjoy it and know that it is fine with you.

AP

The BRF

Magazine

Richard Fisher writes...

For Bible Sunday 2008 we started an initiative called 'The Bible Unwrapped: turn the page'. We offered packs containing sermon notes from David Winter, all-age sketches from the *Barnabas* team, two weeks of Bible readings and more, all to help promote Bible reading. This year, Bible Sunday is on 25 October, and, building on the popularity of the scheme in 2008, we are offering another pack (see the form on page 157 if you would like to order one).

Bible Sunday offers every church a valuable opportunity to encourage Bible reading within their congregation. Such an occasion can be just what is needed to focus attention on this vital aspect of our relationship with God.

Perhaps Bible Sunday will also inspire you to give a lasting gift this Christmas. Your church may appreciate a gift pack of Bible reading notes, Bibles for children or any of the other BRF and Barnabas resources on offer to equip them in their ministry.

Telling people in your church or further afield about your own experience with reading the Bible and how it has impacted on your life may also be a gift you could give. Sharing our stories with family, friends—even those we've just met over coffee after the service—can have a greater effect than we might realise.

In this issue of the BRF Magazine, Ceri Ellis discusses our Quiet Days and Events programme, Lisa Cherrett explains the new direction for our *Guidelines* Bible reading notes, Jane Butcher talks about building a foundation of faith at home and not just at church, Naomi Starkey previews some of our upcoming titles, and there's some exciting news of a major development with our discipleship resource *Foundations21*. There is also an extract from BRF's Advent book for 2009, *Shock and Awe* by Ian Coffey.

Richard Fisher
Chief Executive

A gift to the church

Foundations21
THE NEW WAY TO DO DISCIPLESHIP

Richard Fisher

Earlier this year we began to offer *Foundations21* **free of charge, in place of the previous subscription-based approach. This has been a real step of faith, but it reflects our fundamental desire to make** *Foundations21* **accessible to as many people as possible, as a resource for lifelong Christian learning and discipleship.**

We launched *Foundations21* back in July 2006. Since then, several hundred people have subscribed and more than 1000 people have taken various trial versions. However, although the response from everyone who has seen it has been that it's a remarkable resource, the prevailing view is that content on the web should be free.

Our motivation for developing *Foundations21*, and the motivation of those who so generously funded the project to its launch, was to develop a *new* way of doing discipleship, a *new* way to resource lifelong Christian learning for adults, an approach that embraced the multimedia opportunities offered by the web and was flexible enough to suit different lifestyles as well as different learning styles. No longer would one size have to fit all.

We wrestled for quite some time with the challenge of how to square our vision of making *Foundations21*

available as widely as possible with the need to be able to cover the annual overheads involved. Finally, towards the end of 2008, we took a deep breath and decided to offer *Foundations21* as a gift to the church—free of charge to anyone who wants to use it—and to seek the support of churches, trusts and individuals to secure the funding we need.

At the heart of BRF's ministry is a desire to equip people for Christian living. This involves three strands—helping people to read and understand the Bible, helping them to explore prayer and helping them to grow as disciples of Jesus Christ. *Foundations21* brings all three together.

Through *Foundations21* we want to make a difference and change lives; through *Foundations21* we believe that BRF can make a real contribution towards addressing the challenge in many churches (in the UK and in many other parts of the world) of decreasing levels of biblical and theological literacy. We know that *Foundations21* is making a real difference to people. We have received very moving feedback from a individuals who have shared just how much *Foundations21* has impacted their lives. One subscriber wrote, '*Foundations21* is an answer to prayer! It fits in so well with my family life and I can work through it at my own pace when it is convenient for me to do so.'

By removing the cost factor, we remove what we believe is a significant obstacle preventing the resource from being used more widely. It means we can redirect our energy from focusing on the question 'What is *Foundations21*?' and trying to persuade people to buy it, to asking 'How can you make best use of it?'

This opens up so many opportunities. We are talking to army chaplains, armed forces organisations, workplace ministry organisations, mission organisations, people involved with adult learning, people delivering lay training and continuing ministerial education programmes, vocations advisers, children's advisers and youth organisations. We are currently piloting the use of *Foundations21* in various contexts in three Anglican dioceses and we're talking to numerous other churches and groups. There is considerable interest in *Foundations21* as a resource for small groups, one-to-one mentoring, discipling new Christians, and connecting with those who are dispersed (for example, mission partners and those whose work patterns mean they can't be part of small group life in their church) and people who find it difficult to be part of conventional groups (for example, stroke victims and those with hearing difficulties). There is also interest in the potential for *Foundations21* to be of use within theological colleges in Africa and Asia.

We need to secure at least £65,000 a year to cover the costs of our *Foundations21* ministry and we're seeking funding support for this goal. We believe that support from churches and individuals will grow over time as they make use of *Foundations21* themselves and catch the vision for making it available to others.

Have you had a look at *Foundations21* yourself? Do you know people who might be interested in it? How about your church? Please help us spread the word about it, and let's get as many people as we can engaged in exploring and deepening their relationship with God and becoming even more effective disciples of Jesus Christ.

If you want to find out more or sign up for a copy yourself, you can do so by going to: www.foundations21.org.uk.

Guidelines: the new look

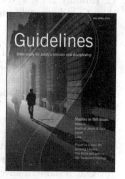

Lisa Cherrett

BRF's *Guidelines* holds a unique position as a series of notes that offers in-depth Bible study of a more scholarly nature than the usual devotional 'thought for the day'. For more than 20 years the notes have been aiming to provoke thought, nourish faith and broaden understanding of the scriptures through the expertise of biblical scholars from the academic world.

From the January–April 2010 issue onward, though, we want to develop *Guidelines* with a more practical, applied approach to theological study. While maintaining the scholarly standard of the writing, we plan to bring in a stronger focus on resourcing those who are meeting the demands of mission and disciple-building in today's church.

Every era brings new challenges to the church. In our own time, we see Christian faith being pushed to the edges rather than acknowledged as central to our culture—and churches are responding with new ways of expressing their witness within the communities they serve. There is a real need for Christian leaders in the church and secular society to

Meeting the demands of mission and disciple-building in today's church

be equipped to guide us into and through these unfamiliar waters, to wrestle with a wide range of practical discipleship issues and to promote a deep understanding of biblical doctrine in an anti-biblical climate.

Those who do not see themselves as leaders, equally, may feel a more urgent desire to boost their confidence in explaining their faith to people whose knowledge of Christian teaching is minimal. They need the tools to think through faith issues for themselves rather than relying on other people's 'easy answers'. Whether we are a minister or lay person, then, each one of us needs to become, like Timothy, 'a worker who does not to need to be ashamed and who correctly handles the word of truth'

(2 Timothy 2:15, TNIV). We hope that *Guidelines* will play a major role in preparing its readers for these challenges.

For the past eight years, Dr Katharine Dell of the University of Cambridge has been responsible for commissioning studies on the Old Testament for *Guidelines*. September–December 2009 is Katharine's last issue as Editor, and we are most grateful to her for the work she has done in bringing the Old Testament alive for the last 24 issues. Many of the letters we've received from *Guidelines* readers over the years have praised the fresh insights into Old Testament books that might seem dry and daunting at first sight. Readers have benefited from Katharine's expertise as a contributor also, especially on the Wisdom writings, and we'd like to thank her and wish her well for the future.

As from January 2010, Canon Dr Jeremy Duff of Liverpool Cathedral, currently New Testament Editor, will become sole Commissioning Editor for *Guidelines*. This does not mean, of course, that the notes will neglect Old Testament study! Like all BRF publications, *Guidelines* remains committed to the whole Bible as a source of inspiration and guidance for everyday life in the church and the world. We also intend to maintain a mixture of systematic study of individual Bible books and thematic study drawing on insights from several books across both Testaments. The Gospels will also continue to be covered in every issue. Strands encompassing mission and leadership, doctrine, church seasons, ethics and cultural issues, as well as prayer and spirituality, will all be woven in, not necessarily in every issue but regularly over the year.

The format of the notes, with weekly sections of six readings plus 'Guidelines', will stay the same, but the covers have been redesigned, using images that are more active, outward-looking and contemporary. We hope that the fresh design will help us to reach new readers as well as continuing to engage the interest of those who have been loyal to *Guidelines* over many years.

The new year kicks off with studies on Luke, Isaiah, Malachi, the death of Jesus in John's Gospel, leadership, the Bible and politics, Old Testament theology and 'prayer in the busyness of life'.

If you would like to receive a complementary copy of *Guidelines Jan–April 2010* to give to your minister, another leader in your church, or someone training for ordination, please phone the BRF office on 01865 319700, or email: enquiries@brf.org.uk.

Lisa Cherrett is BRF's Project Editor and Managing Editor for the Bible reading notes.

BRF's Quiet Days

Ceri Ellis

On an average working day, I will get up, go to work, come home, rush off for some kind of extra-curricular activity—a rehearsal for a concert, a church function, a meal out with friends—and go to bed again. In all the busyness of life, sometimes the only 'quiet time' I can find will be when I'm asleep!

I'm not the only one who has this experience of life: I hear the same story from friends, family, church members and co-workers. It's easy to fill every waking hour with this or that, and not have the chance to just sit, for five minutes or an hour or more, and rest.

BRF's Quiet Days have been running since the late 1990s, giving busy people the opportunity to step out of the race from dawn to dusk and listen to what God is saying. In the first half of 2009 alone, over 200 people have visited different venues around the country to take part in a Quiet Day. 2008 saw over 370 people come to rest in the Lord's presence under the guidance of our experienced speakers.

It has been my job, as Events Coordinator, to plan, book and organise all the Quiet Days since I took up the post in late 2007. The whole experience is enjoyable as I learn more about the events, the venues and the speakers, as well as sometimes getting the chance to meet the people who attend. Since I started, I have attended nine Quiet Days to assist speakers and take part as much as possible throughout the day.

The days usually follow a similar structure, with two sessions led by the speaker in the morning, then lunch and a further session. Each led session is followed by a period of quiet reflection, so the programme is carefully balanced to allow people to spend a significant portion of time listening to God's voice in the silence. Due to our varied list of speakers, including Simon Barrington-Ward, David Winter, Sister Helen Julian CSF and Jennifer Rees Larcombe, the led sessions are always thought-provoking and offer solid teaching on the subject of the day. Many days sell out, but the same level of calm and peace can be found on days with 35 people as on days with smaller numbers.

Each person attending a Quiet

Day will, of course, be affected differently, but I personally have found the days to be spiritually strengthening and an encouragement to my faith. It is surprisingly difficult to sit in quiet contemplation when you are not used to it, but sometimes that is the best way to truly hear what God is saying to us.

Jennifer Rees Larcombe is the author of *Beauty from Ashes* (BRF, 2000) and founder of a charity of the same name, which helps people whose lives have been distorted or broken by loss and trauma. Jennifer has been leading Quiet Days for BRF for many years. She says of the experience:

What always amazes me about Quiet Days is the way they seem to transform the way people look. So often they arrive worn down by life, drained of energy, looking white and strained—just as if they were in need of a good holiday. But when they leave at the end of the day, they look relaxed, rested and radiant—in fact, exactly as if they were returning from their two weeks' annual leave.

The programme for the rest of 2009 features some familiar faces and some new ones. Anne Hibbert is leading a day near Coventry on Proverbs; Maggi Dawn will be drawing on themes from her book *Beginnings and Endings (and what happens in between)* (BRF, 2007) at a day in Cambridgeshire; Ann Persson is speaking on the theme 'Invitation' near Henley-on-Thames in Oxfordshire. With Quiet Days and events stretching from September to December, there are many different themes and venues to choose from.

We also offer advice for people wishing to run Quiet Days of their own in their local area. We can advertise days like these on our website and through the special Quiet Days emailing list, which currently goes out to around 300 people. Through the Quiet Spaces website, you can find a set of guidelines on how to organise your own Quiet Day, covering everything from finding a speaker to arranging catering for the day. So if there isn't a BRF Quiet Day happening near you, why not consider hosting one of your own? Visit www.quietspaces.org.uk for more details, or contact the office on 01865 319700.

Our Quiet Day programme for 2009 is available in print from BRF. To request a print copy or to book a place on a Quiet Day, call 01865 319700 or write to the usual BRF address. You can also view the programme and book places online at www.quietspaces.org.uk/events.

Ceri Ellis is BRF's Events and Direct Marketing Coordinator. In her spare time, she enjoys writing novels, reading novels and singing.

Barnabas in Churches: what, how, when, why?

Jane Butcher

The heart of Barnabas in Churches is captured in the tagline 'Resourcing children's work in churches'. The form that takes can vary: it can involve direct contact with a church, either leading or working alongside a church team to run events such as *The Christmas Journey* or holiday Bible clubs, or running training events for an individual or group of churches. It can also entail leading sessions at Diocesan or ecumenical events that offer training and support for those involved in children's ministry.

Even when the *Barnabas* team cannot meet children's leaders face to face, we can offer other resources. There is a wealth of free, downloadable ideas on our website www.barnabasinchurches.org.uk and, of course, Barnabas publishes a range of written resources to assist children's ministry.

However, we are increasingly aware of the need to think outside the box regarding what 'church' looks like in today's society. Much research confirms the idea that Sunday, for many people, has changed in its style, and church is no longer part of the picture. This raises the question of whether there is a need to consider 'church outside Sunday' or 'midweek church'—a concept that is highlighted by the work of Fresh Expressions (see the website www.freshexpressions.org.uk). Messy Church is one example of a Fresh Expression of church, developed by Lucy Moore, a member of the *Barnabas* team. To find out more, do take a look at the website www.messychurch.org.uk.

But is faith development the role of the church alone (or, more particularly, the church and Sunday school leaders)? Maybe we need to look to the African proverb, 'It takes a village to raise a child.' If we transfer this idea to church, perhaps it indicates that the wider church has a role in nurturing children. It highlights the richness of relationships that can exist among people of all ages, genders and backgrounds. Are there church members who have experiences and abilities they could share with others? For example, could those with knitting, crochet or other craft skills visit the toddler or preschool groups to teach others? Are there people—teenagers or adults—with musical ability who could offer to do some singing at children's groups? These and many other possibilities allow shared experiences to enhance our relationships and our sense of belonging to the church family of which we are a part.

In addition, the *Barnabas* team has been considering how faith development can take place in the home—how all members of a family can experience and develop in their faith together. The church has been so long accustomed to being the focal point, as far as teaching and learning is concerned, that it really is hard to get out of that mindset, and we may rarely hear 'faith in the home' preached about. However, various pieces of research have confirmed that children are most influenced by their parent(s) or carer(s) and that the home is a significant place of learning.

This being the case, it suggests that home can offer an environment in which to enhance the development of faith. For many adults, however, this may raise some 'how' questions. How do you pray with children? How do you tell Bible stories with words that children can understand? How can we do activities that involve children of various ages?

One response would be to highlight the wealth of ideas that are now freely available on websites and in books and Bibles written specifically for children. In particular, there are many ways in which festivals and the everyday things of life can be used to help focus the thoughts of all family members and stimulate discussion.

For example, why not make a 'family favourites picture collage', allowing each person to contribute photographs, postcards or other items that remind them of a favourite time—maybe from the summer holidays or Christmas, or events in the last academic or calendar year. The collage can then be used as a springboard into prayer. Each day, possibly at breakfast or after an evening meal together, a different person could take a turn to point out their item, explain why it is special and thank God for that time.

There are many other activities that can draw on the everyday experiences of life to enhance the development of faith in people of all ages. What is important is for children and adults alike to experience significant opportunities that allow us all to draw closer to God and allow him to draw near to us.

Jane Butcher is a member of the Barnabas *team, based in the Midlands.*

The Editor recommends

Naomi Starkey

As the Bible Reading Fellowship, it is (to state the obvious) central to everything we do that we encourage people to read the Bible, to understand what they are reading, and to see how they can apply it to their lives. Reading the Bible, though, is not like reading any other book. Not only is it longer than most books (and the paper thinner and the print smaller) but, as we continue as Christian disciples, we find ourselves reading and rereading the same passages. It can be hard to carry on seeking new insights from a particular set of verses when we feel we know them inside out and back to front.

Over-familiarity can be a problem for preachers, too, particularly at Easter and Christmas, when the season demands the same sermon topic every year. Of course we can pray for the inspiration of the Holy Spirit, but we may still find it a real struggle to come up with an inspiring message, especially if the congregation is more or less still the same (and will eventually have heard all our best anecdotes and illustrations!).

Much of our publishing at BRF—both books and Bible reading notes—is geared to helping people reencounter familiar texts. It's not that the meaning itself has changed, but there may be unexpected connections, helpful applications and imaginative ways of accessing the original power of the passages. *The Real Godsend* by Dr Nigel G. Wright is subtitled 'Preaching the birth narratives in Matthew and Luke', which sums up the book's aim: bringing out the powerful witness of what are probably the most familiar of all Bible passages.

The accounts of Jesus' birth tend to be seen as 'Christmas stories', overlaid with seasonal trimmings that, as often as not, stifle rather than clarify their meaning. *The Real Godsend* shows how we can preach and teach these well-known and well-loved narratives, revealing them as carefully crafted works of theology, written in the light of the resurrection and drawing on the Hebrew scriptures (the Old Testament) to reveal the nature of the God who sent his Son into the world.

At the same time, Nigel Wright

shows how these accounts do not simply relate ancient history but invite us to believe in the risen Christ who is alive now, the real Godsend who comes to us as God's greatest gift. Understanding the narratives at a deeper level means that we can use their vivid imagery and richly textured themes to communicate these most profound of truths.

In writing this book, Nigel Wright draws on a wealth of academic and pastoral experience. He is Principal of Spurgeon's College, London, a former president of the Baptist Union of Great Britain, and has also worked in two churches in the north of England. He has written extensively on issues of church renewal and has also written *God on the Inside: the Holy Spirit in Holy Scripture* for BRF.

While the Old Testament is less well-known, in general, than the New, one story that remains a perennial favourite is David and Goliath. The idea of the 'little man' who, despite inadequate weaponry, manages to kill the 'giant' is part of popular culture, as well as being reflected in this story in scripture, but too often it ends up being seen as more suitable for Sunday school material than as a topic for mature reflection. In *Confidence in the Living God*, Bishop Andrew Watson revisits the David and Goliath episode, using a narrative theology approach to reveal an underlying theme of confidence.

Confidence lies at the heart of our society, determining the success or failure of the economy, the government, companies, schools and churches. It also profoundly affects individual lives, whether we are members of a sports team, part of a business consortium or facing a major exam. As Christians, we are called to proclaim our faith in the living God, but how can we build this confidence in a culture where such faith is often dismissed as embarrassing or even downright dangerous?

Working systematically through the events of the Bible story as they unfold, Bishop Andrew not only provides useful background on the characters and historical context, but also shows how confidence is a central theme—and how it relates to our lives today. He reflects on God's ability to develop a proper self-confidence within individuals and his Church, so as to reveal the gospel through transforming words and transformed lives.

Confidence in the Living God is Bishop Andrew's second book for BRF, following *The Fourfold Leadership of Jesus* (2008). As Bishop of Aston he is involved in promoting church growth and leadership across the diocese of Birmingham. He was previously vicar of St Stephen's, East Twickenham, where he helped pioneer three church plants.

To order a copy of any of these books, please turn to the order form on page 159.

A extract from
Shock and Awe

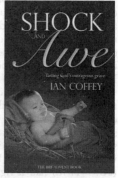

In BRF's Advent book for 2009, author Ian Coffey explores our amazing, all-loving, all-powerful God and how he reaches out to save us—if we only put our trust in him. Starting with Abraham and concluding with the heavenly vision of Revelation, *Shock and Awe* reflects on some of the gifts that grace brings and shows what it means practically to live as followers of Christ and as people of hope. The following extract is an abridged version of the Introduction and the first day's reading.

Introduction

Advent is a season of surprise.

The Bible readings and meditations in this book will regularly remind us that the incarnation of Jesus Christ, God's Son, was met with incredulity, wonder and astonishment… When I began to think about these Advent readings and how we might rediscover the wonder of the incarnation, I was gripped by a phrase that wouldn't let go of me: 'shock and awe'.

Mention the words 'shock and awe' to many people and they are instantly connected with the contentious military campaign launched against Iraq in 2003. But the phrase itself was borrowed by military commanders from a strategy developed some years previously at the National Defense University of the United States of America.

Two military strategists observed a lesson from history, stretching back many centuries: put simply, if you can overwhelm your enemy with an early strike of decisive force, then their will to resist is broken. By the process of shock, your opponent is awed into submission.

Leaving aside the controversy surrounding the decision to invade Iraq (a valid and important discussion for another place), I was struck by the description 'shock and awe' and the tacit assumption that this could only be achieved by bombs, bullets, might and power.

The kingdom of God is about shock and awe, but of a wholly different kind. The gospel of the Lord Jesus Christ is of a king who stoops to conquer, who washes the feet of his followers, takes the place of a lowly slave and is willing to pay the ultimate price of redeeming love through an ignominious and unjust death. There is no apparent might or power in a baby in a manger, or a man riding on a donkey surrounded by cheering children, or one nailed to a cross before a jeering crowd. But the important word here is 'apparent'.

The shock of the incarnation of the servant-king has led to a different kind of awe—not that of the subjugated, terrorised and submissive, but rather the awe of wonder, incredulity and love. Isaac Watts (1674–1748) had it right when he wrote that nothing in the whole of creation could respond to such amazing love without the giving of its whole self to God in grateful submission and service…

The big story of the Bible speaks of God's great rescue project for lost people. The theme of the story is grace (undeserved love) and his method, shock and awe. This is a God of surprises who chooses unlikely people and works in unusual ways. Our studies through this season of Advent will help us dip into that story and see firsthand what it involves.

We begin with Abram in the first book of the Bible, Genesis, and we conclude with a vision of God's future plan in the final book of Revelation. In between, we shall consider what it means to be people of faith, trusting God's promises and encountering him in new ways in our daily lives. We shall consider some of the gifts that grace brings and think about what it means practically to live as followers of Christ and as people of hope. It's my hope that this will be a positive learning experience as the Spirit of God impresses and underlines truth for us. I am reminded of Mohandas Gandhi's advice: 'Live as if you were to die tomorrow. Learn as if you were to live for ever'.

The studies have been prepared on the basis of daily readings over the six weeks of Advent, but a study guide has been included for those who may wish to compare notes with a wider group.

My prayer is that these studies will give us a deeper glimpse of what it means to taste outrageous grace and to live in the good of it… Let's explore this outrageous grace.

1 December: Faith that walks

READ GENESIS 12:1–5

My wife and I lived abroad for several years. I remember the work involved in moving—finding the best removal company, organising a house to rent, opening bank accounts, locating doctors and dentists, insuring the car—and all in a foreign language. We are glad we did it as the experience brought many good things—not least the capacity to empathise with anyone who announces, 'I am moving to work abroad.'

Abram faced a much bigger challenge. God asked him to set out for an unknown destination. His family had lived in the city of Ur (11:31), located in the region we know as southern Iraq. God had begun to speak to Abram and told him to leave everything familiar and secure and set out for somewhere better, yet to be revealed.

Abram and his family settled for a time in a place called Haran, a bustling caravan city. The Bible doesn't tell us why he took the decision to stay there: it may have been due to circumstances beyond his control. During this time, his father Terah died and Abram and his entourage then journeyed on towards the land of Canaan. This sets the scene for the remarkable promise that God gave to Abram—a promise that has implications for us as well.

It is not clear from Genesis when the promise was made—it could date back to the time when he was living in Ur—but the details are very clear. The promise is made up of seven strands set out in our reading.

- From Abram will come a great nation.
- Abram will be blessed by God.
- Abram's name will be made great.
- He will be a blessing.
- Those who bless him (treat him well) will be blessed by God.
- Those who curse him (treat him badly) will be cursed by God.
- All peoples on earth will be blessed through Abram.

I can't begin to imagine the impact this news must have had on Abram. My mind is filled with questions.

How did he know that this was God speaking and not his overactive imagination? Did he tell his wife and family about the promise? Did he have doubts on the journey? What did his friends in Ur and Haran say about the move?

The Bible doesn't answer my questions but leaves me with this faith-filled phrase: 'So Abram left, as the Lord had told him' (v. 4). That's all I need to know. Abram's faith led to obedient action, and that meant taking a long walk to a new place that God would show him at some future date.

We sometimes make the mistake of thinking that everything needs to be mapped out and planned before we take the step of faith. If that were so, then faith would not be necessary as the path ahead would be obvious. Faith means trusting God when sometimes all we can see is the next step. As we take that step, we trust that the next one will become visible.

Is there a step of faith and obedience that you need to take? Let Abram's example inspire you.

Reflect

'We live by faith, not by sight' (2 Corinthians 5:7).

Father God, teach me to walk by faith, trusting completely in your fatherly care. Amen

To order a copy of this book, please turn to the order form on page 159.

New Daylight © BRF 2009

The Bible Reading Fellowship
15 The Chambers, Vineyard, Abingdon OX14 3FE
Tel: 01865 319700; Fax: 01865 319701
E-mail: enquiries@brf.org.uk; Website: www.brf.org.uk

ISBN 978 1 84101 521 7

Distributed in Australia by:
Willow Connection, PO Box 288, Brookvale, NSW 2100.
Tel: 02 9948 3957; Fax: 02 9948 8153;
E-mail: info@willowconnection.com.au
Available also from all good Christian bookshops in Australia.
For individual and group subscriptions in Australia:
Mrs Rosemary Morrall, PO Box W35, Wanniassa, ACT 2903.

Distributed in New Zealand by:
Scripture Union Wholesale, PO Box 760, Wellington
Tel: 04 385 0421; Fax: 04 384 3990; E-mail: suwholesale@clear.net.nz

Distributed in Canada by:
The Anglican Book Centre, 80 Hayden Street, Toronto, Ontario, M4Y 3G2
Tel: 001 416 924-1332; Fax: 001 416 924-2760;
E-mail: abc@anglicanbookcentre.com; Website: www.anglicanbookcentre.com

Publications distributed to more than 60 countries

Acknowledgments

Printed in Singapore by Craft Print International Ltd

SUPPORTING BRF'S MINISTRY

As a Christian charity, BRF is involved in five distinct yet complementary areas. Through our **BRF** ministry (www.brf.org.uk), we're resourcing adults for their spiritual journey through Bible reading notes, books, and a programme of quiet days and teaching days. BRF also provides the infrastructure that supports our other four specialist ministries.

Our **Foundations21** ministry (www.foundations21.org.uk) is providing flexible and innovative ways for individuals and groups to explore their Christian faith and discipleship through a multimedia internet-based resource.

Led by Lucy Moore, our **Messy Church** ministry is enabling churches all over the UK (and increasingly abroad) to reach children and adults beyond the fringes of the church (visit www.messychurch.org.uk).

Through our **Barnabas in Churches** ministry, we're helping churches to support, resource and develop their children's ministry with the under-11s more effectively (visit www.barnabasinchurches.org.uk).

Our **Barnabas in Schools** ministry (www.barnabasinschools.org.uk) is enabling primary school children and teachers to explore Christianity creatively and bring the Bible alive within RE and Collective Worship.

At the heart of BRF's ministry is a desire to equip adults and children for Christian living—helping them to read and understand the Bible, to explore prayer and to grow as disciples of Jesus. In an increasingly secular world, people need this help more than ever. We can do something about it, but our resources are limited. We need your help to make a real impact on the local church, local schools and the wider community.

- You could support BRF's ministry with a donation or standing order (using the response form overleaf).
- You could consider making a bequest to BRF in your will. (We have a leaflet available with more information about this, which can be requested using the form overleaf.)
- You could encourage your church to support BRF as part of your church's giving to home mission—perhaps focusing on a specific area of our ministry, or a particular member of our *Barnabas* team.
- Most important of all, you could support BRF with your prayers.

If you would like to discuss how a specific gift or bequest could be used in the development of our ministry, Chief Executive Richard Fisher would be delighted to talk further with you, either on the telephone or in person. Please let us know if you would like him to contact you.

Whatever you can do or give, we thank you for your support.

BRF MINISTRY APPEAL RESPONSE FORM

Name _____

Address _____

_____ Postcode _____

Telephone _____ Email _____

(tick as appropriate)

Gift Aid Declaration

☐ I am a UK taxpayer. I want BRF to treat as Gift Aid Donations all donations I make from 6 April 2000 until I notify you otherwise.

Signature _____ Date _____

☐ I would like to support BRF's ministry with a regular donation by standing order (please complete the Banker's Order below).

Standing Order – Banker's Order

To the Manager, Name of Bank/Building Society _____

Address _____

_____ Postcode _____

Sort Code _____ Account Name _____

Account No _____

Please pay Royal Bank of Scotland plc, Drummonds, 49 Charing Cross, London SW1A 2DX (Sort Code 16-00-38), for the account of BRF A/C No. 00774151

The sum of _____ pounds on ___ /___ /___ (insert date your standing order starts) and thereafter the same amount on the same day of each month until further notice.

Signature _____ Date _____

Single donation

☐ I enclose my cheque/credit card/Switch card details for a donation of £5 £10 £25 £50 £100 £250 (other) £ _____ to support BRF's ministry

Credit/Switch card no. ☐☐☐☐☐☐☐☐☐☐☐☐☐☐☐☐☐☐☐☐

Expires ☐☐☐☐ Security code ☐☐☐ Issue no. of Switch card ☐☐☐☐

Signature _____ Date _____

(Where appropriate, on receipt of your donation, we will send you a Gift Aid form)

☐ Please send me information about making a bequest to BRF in my will.

Please detach and send this completed form to: Richard Fisher, BRF, 15 The Chambers, Vineyard, Abingdon OX14 3FE. BRF is a Registered Charity (No.233280)

ND0309

BIBLE READING RESOURCES PACK

An updated pack of resources and ideas to help to promote Bible reading in your church is available from BRF. The pack, which will be of use at any time during the year (but especially for Bible Sunday in October), includes sample readings from BRF's Bible reading notes and *The People's Bible Commentary*, a sermon outline, an all-age sketch, a children's activity, information about BRF's ministry and much more.

Unless you specify the month in which you would like the pack sent, we will send it immediately on receipt of your order. We greatly appreciate your donations towards the cost of producing the pack (without them we would not be able to make the pack available) and we welcome your comments about the contents of the pack and your ideas for future ones.

This coupon should be sent to:

**BRF
15 The Chambers
Vineyard
Abingdon
OX14 3FE**

Name ⎯⎯⎯⎯⎯⎯⎯⎯⎯⎯⎯⎯⎯⎯⎯⎯⎯⎯⎯⎯

Address ⎯⎯⎯⎯⎯⎯⎯⎯⎯⎯⎯⎯⎯⎯⎯⎯⎯⎯⎯⎯

⎯⎯⎯⎯⎯⎯⎯⎯⎯⎯⎯⎯⎯⎯⎯ Postcode ⎯⎯⎯⎯⎯⎯

Telephone ⎯⎯⎯⎯⎯⎯⎯⎯⎯⎯⎯⎯⎯⎯⎯⎯⎯⎯⎯

Email ⎯⎯⎯⎯⎯⎯⎯⎯⎯⎯⎯⎯⎯⎯⎯⎯⎯⎯⎯⎯

Please send me ⎯⎯⎯⎯ Bible Reading Resources Pack(s)

Please send the pack now/ in ⎯⎯⎯⎯⎯⎯⎯⎯ (month).

I enclose a donation for £ ⎯⎯⎯⎯ towards the cost of the pack.

BRF is a Registered Charity

❏ Please send me a Bible reading resources pack
❏ I would like to take out a subscription myself (complete your name and address details only once)
❏ I would like to give a gift subscription (please complete both name and address sections below)

Your name _____

Your address _____

_____Postcode _____

Gift subscription name _____

Gift subscription address _____

_____Postcode _____

Gift message (20 words max.) _____

_____

Please send *New Daylight* beginning with the January / May / September 2010 issue: (delete as applicable)

(please tick box)	UK	SURFACE	AIR MAIL
NEW DAYLIGHT	❏ £13.80	❏ £15.00	❏ £17.10
NEW DAYLIGHT 3-year sub	❏ £33.00		
NEW DAYLIGHT DELUXE	❏ £17.40	❏ £21.90	❏ £27.00
NEW DAYLIGHT daily email only	❏ £12.00		
NEW DAYLIGHT email + printed	❏ £21.60		

Your email address _____

Please complete the payment details below and send, with appropriate payment, to: **BRF, 15 The Chambers, Vineyard, Abingdon OX14 3FE.**

Total enclosed £ _____ (cheques should be made payable to 'BRF')

Payment by cheque ❏ postal order ❏ Visa ❏ Mastercard ❏ Switch ❏

Card number: ☐☐☐☐☐☐☐☐☐☐☐☐☐☐☐☐☐☐

Expires: ☐☐☐☐   Security code ☐☐☐   Issue no (Switch): ☐☐☐

Signature (essential if paying by credit/Switch) _____

BRF is a Registered Charity

BRF PUBLICATIONS ORDER FORM

Please ensure that you complete and send off both sides of this order form.

Please send me the following book(s):

		Quantity	Price	Total

Books for Advent and Christmas:

641 2	Shock and Awe (*I. Coffey*)	_____	£6.99	_____
247 6	A Handful of Light (*M. Mitton*)	_____	£7.99	_____
566 8	Beginnings and Endings (*M. Dawn*)	_____	£7.99	_____
677 1	Five Impossible Things to Believe before Christmas (*K. Scully*)	_____	£5.99	_____
705 1	Silent Night (*V. Howie*)	_____	£7.99	_____
585 9	Easy Ways to Christmas Plays 2 (*V. Howie*)	_____	£11.99	_____
623 8	Looking Forward to Christmas with Timothy Bear (*B. Sears*)	_____	£7.99	_____
684 9	Christmas Sticker Collection (*S. Box*)	_____	£3.99	_____
621 4	The Christmas Journey (*M. Curry & G. Morgan*)	_____	£6.99	_____

Recommended books/authors in this issue

707 5	The Barnabas Classic Children's Bible (*R. Davies*)	_____	£11.99	_____
576 7	The Real Godsend (*N. Wright*)	_____	£7.99	_____
484 5	God on the Inside (*N. Wright*)	_____	£7.99	_____
643 6	Confidence in the Living God (*A. Watson*)	_____	£7.99	_____
435 7	The Fourfold Leadership of Jesus (*A. Watson*)	_____	£7.99	_____
071 7	PBC: Proverbs (*E.B. Mellor*)	_____	£7.99	_____
087 8	PBC: Jeremiah (*R. Mason*)	_____	£7.99	_____
012 0	PBC: Galatians and 1 & 2 Thessalonians (*J. Fenton*)	_____	£7.99	_____
092 2	PBC: James to Jude (*F.J. Moloney*)	_____	£7.99	_____

Total cost of books £ _____

Donation £ _____

Postage and packing £ _____

TOTAL £ _____

POSTAGE AND PACKING CHARGES				
order value	UK	Europe	Surface	Air Mail
£7.00 & under	£1.25	£3.00	£3.50	£5.50
£7.01–£30.00	£2.25	£5.50	£6.50	£10.00
Over £30.00	free	prices on request		

See over for payment details. All prices are correct at time of going to press, are subject to the prevailing rate of VAT and may be subject to change without prior warning.

Please complete the payment details below and send with appropriate payment and completed order form to:

**BRF, 15 The Chambers, Vineyard,
Abingdon OX14 3FE**

Name _____

Address _____

_____

_____ Postcode _____

Telephone _____

Email _____

Total enclosed £ _____(cheques should be made payable to 'BRF')

Payment by cheque ❏ postal order ❏ Visa ❏ Mastercard ❏ Switch ❏

Card number: ⬜⬜⬜⬜⬜⬜⬜⬜⬜⬜⬜⬜⬜⬜⬜⬜

Expires: ⬜⬜⬜⬜ Security code ⬜⬜⬜ Issue no (Switch): ⬜⬜⬜⬜

Signature (essential if paying by credit/Switch card)_____

❏ Please do not send me further information about BRF publications.

ALTERNATIVE WAYS TO ORDER

Christian bookshops: All good Christian bookshops stock BRF publications. For your nearest stockist, please contact BRF.

Telephone: The BRF office is open between 09.15 and 17.30.
To place your order, phone 01865 319700; fax 01865 319701.

Web: Visit www.brf.org.uk

BRF is a Registered Charity

ND0309